NAMES DON'T HAVE A GENDER

By Steph Coffield

ISBN-13: 979-8-218-07031-1

First edition, October 2022

Laura,
Thank you for wearing all the hats and the best friend hat
most of all.

TABLE OF CONTENTS

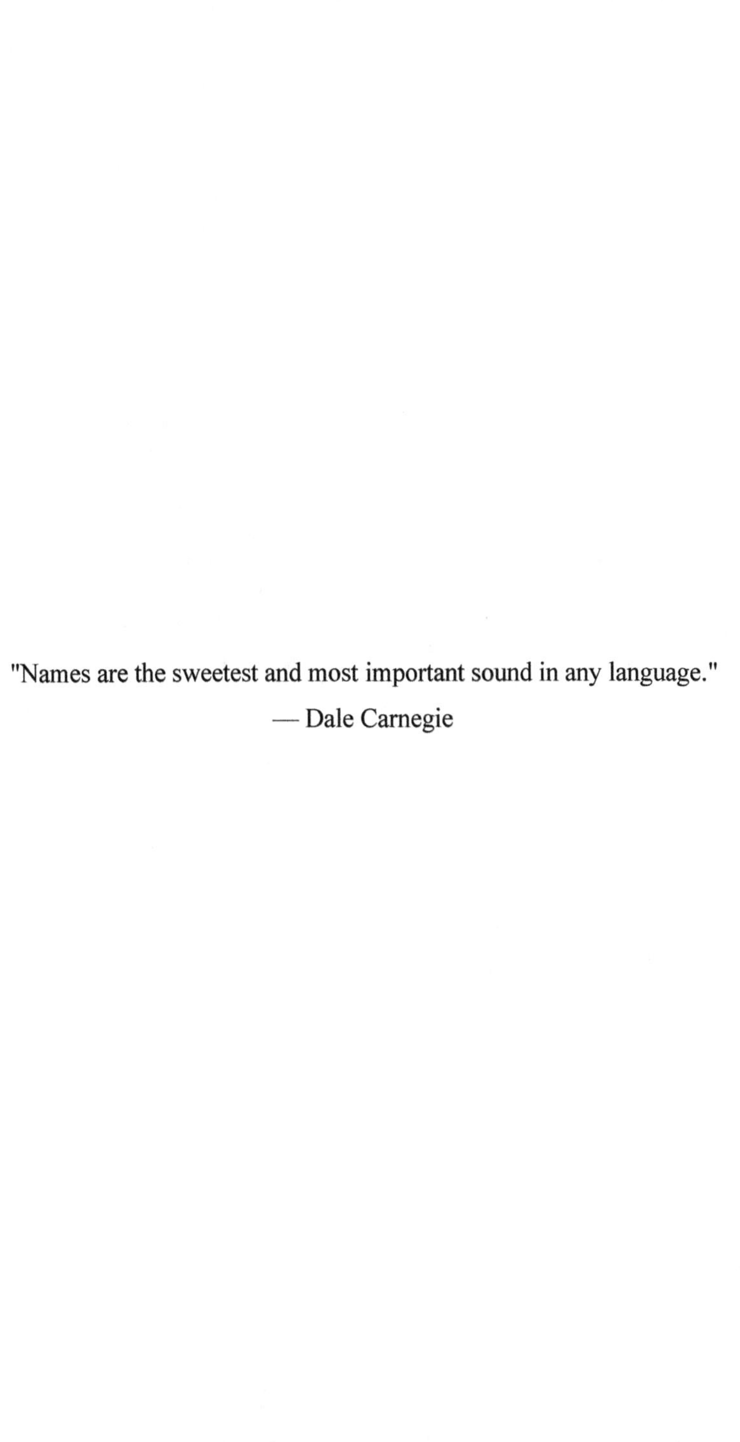

"Names are the sweetest and most important sound in any language."

— Dale Carnegie

INTRODUCTION

WHEN YOU MEET SOMEONE new, what is the first thing you ask them? "What's your name," right? Asking for someone's name is our way of learning a small but intimate detail about another person to aid in our familiarity with them. A name can give you insight into someone's culture, their style, and oftentimes, their personality. Names can be invisible strings that attach a person to distant family members many generations back or to a complete stranger upon realizing a name is shared. Unique and special stories live behind a person's name, and they are symbols of love, strength, beauty, and resilience.

I like to joke about how easy it was for me to name a child before getting pregnant. There is a carefree quietness in naming a *future* child; you can daydream about all the options and change your direction on a whim without consequence. But when you are suddenly faced with naming an actual person, a human being with their own life story and purpose, the pressure begins to mount. If I have learned anything as a name consultant these past years, it's that you are not alone in wanting to find the perfect name for your little one. You are not alone if you are struggling to make a decision or if you can't agree with your partner. I promise the perfect name for your family DOES exist, and my hope is that maybe you find it in this book.

This book is a compilation of my favorite names from a myriad of different themes. Each one of them has been handpicked to live on these pages as inspiration for you.

There are no boy and girl name lists in this book. Don't misunderstand me; there are definitely names that I view as more feminine and names I view as more masculine, but those are simply my opinions and/or society's traditions. Truly, names don't have a gender. The ultimate goal is to choose a name that grabs you, makes you smile, and fits perfectly in your family.

At the end of this book, there are a few pages for you to create lists of your favorite names. May I suggest using a pencil? I found that my baby name lists were always changing.

A note on sharing names from different cultures: I am only able to write this book through the lens of a privileged white girl of mixed European descent living in America. I intentionally limited the number of names I shared from non-white cultures because oftentimes, those names are meant to stay inside of those cultures. I recognize the weight my name suggestions might have on my readers, and I ask that you take a name's origin into consideration before using it.

A note on choosing a new name for yourself: This book is perfect for trans people, non-binary folks, and anyone else who is searching for a new moniker. While there are lots of references to naming a baby in this book, it's only because that is where my experience comes from and what I do in most of my name orders on Fiverr. But please know this book has been written with you in mind since its conception. This name book is perfect for anyone who is gender-fluid or who doesn't want to limit themselves with the traditional boy and girl lists.

A note for my authors out there: This book is great for naming characters in novels and for keeping track of the names you have already used. I hear from authors all the time about how they've found a name for their characters in one of my TikTok videos and that makes me just as happy as when I help someone name their baby.

A note on names for pet and plant lovers: This book can help you name your furbaby or your fiddle fig tree and I'm here for it. A great name can make any bond that much closer.

Expecting parents are not the only ones looking for fun, unusual, and uncommon names, and I'm glad you're reading this book, no matter the reason.

Now for my disclaimer. While I did my absolute best to make sure that all of the name origins and meanings in this book are correct, I am not able to guarantee every single fact in this book. I relied heavily, but not exclusively, on Nameberry.com and BabyNames.com, and I thank them for their extensive lists of names. Take note that many names will have different meanings in different languages, and it's difficult to include every origin of every name.

This book is not a replacement for doing your own name research. It is ultimately your responsibility to understand the background and meaning of the name you choose. *Names Don't Have a Gender* is a tool for you to explore names in a new way that has not been done before. There are no long lists in this book. There are no name repeats. Names are categorized subjectively by me based on how often I see them being used. Therefore they are considered popular or uncommon. I chose my absolute favorite names for each of these fifty-seven categories, and I'm so excited for you to see them too.

MY NAMING JOURNEY

ALL THREE OF MY children were named in the eleventh hour, at the very end of my pregnancies. While I definitely felt the weight of the responsibility of choosing a name, I never actually felt rushed. In fact, I almost prolonged my decision so that I could continue indulging in all of the name books, websites, and YouTube videos. I wanted to see every name out there and ponder every possibility.

Our starting point for names was based on the fact that my husband is from Glasgow, Scotland, and since we were going to be raising our family in the United States, we wanted to highlight our children's Scottish side with Gaelic or Celtic baby names. Funnily enough, the Celtic theme is strong in my first child's name but basically non-existent by our third kiddo.

In the course of my first pregnancy, my husband and I moved from Kansas City to the Minneapolis-St. Paul area of Minnesota and then from my parent's house into our first home. We were living on one income, had one vehicle, and just enough money to pay our bills with no room for anything else. I spent my days walking the dog, blogging, prepping for baby, organizing our house, and of course, scouring the web for the perfect baby name.

We knew we were having a boy, and we knew we wanted a

name that had a special meaning to us. Our shortlist was nothing I'd recognize today; It was pretty traditional and not very uncommon. My taste has definitely evolved.

The original list included Scottish names as well as some Norse names from my Scandinavian heritage:

- Gavin
- Logan
- Scott
- Jari
- Brant
- Loki

One day while I was scrolling a Celtic boy list over lunch, I saw the name Euan. It jumped off the page at me, and immediately, I was in love. I sent my husband a message and asked him what he thought of the name… he liked it! Now my hubby is the king of the name veto, so this was pretty exciting.

Euan means 'born of the yew tree', which is a lovely nature inspired meaning, but it wasn't the special reason we picked it for his name. Euan is a variation of the name John, and consequently my husband's name Iain (pronounced Ian). His parents chose Iain because it is the Gaelic version of John. The traditional Scottish spelling is actually Ewan, but we chose Euan because I liked the idea of both father and son having three vowels in their four letter names.

Our sweet baby Euan was immediately connected to his father and his Scottish grandpa. But what about my Dad? Well, another version of Euan is the Irish name Eoghan, and I found some information online that Eoghan is similar to the name Eugene. My Dad's name is Gene. So no matter how thin the rope may be, our eldest's name is tied to his father and *both* grandpas, which I absolutely love. The only problem would be if we had another boy, finding a name I loved just as much.

Cut to my second pregnancy, and surprise; we're having a boy! Brothers only a year and a half apart! I was a new mom with no time to research baby names and no idea how I was going to find another Celtic name with as much meaning to us as Euan. Not only that, but we had given my very unique maiden name to my oldest son as well, and I couldn't figure out for the life of me why I couldn't do that again, so we did.

Now we had a middle name but no first name until one night Iain and I were chatting before bed, and he randomly suggested the name, Fitz. Not Fitzgerald or Fitzwilliams, but plainly and sweetly, Fitz.

I quickly went to look it up and found that Fitz means 'son of.' Fitz's name would then be the son of my family name (middle name) and my husband's family name (last name). It was perfect, very meaningful, and had four letters, just like his brother's name. I was sold.

In true middle kid fashion, I don't have a list of baby names saved from my second pregnancy. Looking back, it appears I named our first kid, and my husband named our second kid, so who would name kiddo number three? Truthfully we weren't sure we were going to have a third for many years but guess who got baby fever…

The decision to have a third child was not easy for our family. Iain and I were divided for a long time. He wanted to stick with two, and I was becoming desperate for a third. We didn't know how to make such a major life decision while acknowledging each other's needs and wants. After many long and candid conversations, debating pros and cons, and a lot of patience, we both decided to go forward with having another child.

It was about this time that I discovered baby name videos on YouTube. Shout out to SJ Strum; her channel was everything to me at the time! I became hyper-focused on uncommon names that no one else was giving their child. My husband, on the other hand, was completely the opposite. He enjoyed classic names. Euan is a unique name in America but a very popular name for him growing up in Scotland. To this day, I still don't know how he came up with a name as cool and uncommon as Fitz because he shot down practically every quirky name I've ever suggested.

This time we weren't going to find out the baby's sex. Despite a high-risk pregnancy and tons of extra ultrasounds, we did not find out what we were having until baby arrived, and it was the best surprise.

I had always wanted a daughter, but the joy of having sons was like nothing I could have ever imagined, and I happily dreamed about three Coffield boys. It felt like we were destined to have boys. But when it came to another special boy name, we were lost YET AGAIN. After accidentally naming two boys with an E and F, I was determined to come up with a G name for potential baby boy number three.

Our shortlist for boys included:

- Gage (yay for a four letter G name)
- Vonn
- Mack (another name that means 'son of')
- Quill (this ended up being our top contender for a couple of reasons)

For girl names, we were also starting at the beginning because despite being set on Isla for more than five years, suddenly it was quite popular and much less appealing. I'm not saying its popularity was the only reason we let it go, but it was a contributing factor. The other reason was that we simply felt less attached to it and wanted to explore other options.

Our short list for girls included:

- Fallon
- Teagan
- Saffron
- Long list of names that start with Ori

I guess this is a good time to say technically, we both named our third child. Iain came to me with the nickname Ori from a video game he played and I said YES, but she'll need a full name. My goal was to find a long form of the adorable nickname Ori. Here's what we had:

Orianna Lynn Coffield- golden dawn

Orietta Lynn Coffield- golden, beautiful

Oribella Lynn Coffield- beautiful, golden child

Orianne Lynn Coffield- dawn, gold, sunrise

Orianthi Lynn Coffield- beautiful flower

After a precipitous labor and birth, our precious baby girl was born and we named her Orianna Lynn Coffield. The Anna in her name is pronounced like AH-nuh and I will probably correct you if you say ANN-uh. The coolest part? She shares a middle name with my mother and I. The three generations being Vicky Lynn, Stephanie Lynn, and Orianna Lynn. I couldn't love it more.

ANIMALS

<u>Popular</u>

☐	**Bear**	Old English	carnivorous mammal
☐	**Bee**	Latin	she who brings happiness, insect
☐	**Buck**	Old English	males of many horned animals
☐	**Colt**	English	young male horse
☐	**Drake**	Old English	male duck
☐	**Doe**	English, Norman	female deer
☐	**Kit**	Greek, English	young fur-bearing animal
☐	**Fawn**	French, English	a young deer
☐	**Fox**	Old English	wild animal in dog family
☐	**Wolf**	German	wolf

<u>Uncommon</u>

☐	**Anemone**	Greek	windflower, marine animal
☐	**Jaguar**	Tupi and Guarani	he who kills with one leap, large cat
☐	**Lynx**	Greek	brightness
☐	**Otter**	German, Dutch	otter
☐	**Panda**	Nepalese	bamboo eater, giant bear
☐	**Pike**	English	pike, a fish
☐	**Puma**	Latin	Mountain lion
☐	**Sable**	Slavic	black
☐	**Seal**	English	dweller by the small wood, marine mammal
☐	**Shark**	Middle English	shark

ASTRONOMY

Popular

- ☐ **Atlas** — Greek — to endure, to carry
- ☐ **Cosmos** — Greek — order, organization, beauty
- ☐ **Comet** — Word name — large objects of dust and ice that orbit the sun
- ☐ **Luna** — Latin — moon
- ☐ **Mars** — Roman — god of war, planet name
- ☐ **Nova** — Latin — astronomical event that causes a new star
- ☐ **Orion** — Greek — constellation name
- ☐ **Polaris** — Latin — north star
- ☐ **Skye** — Scottish — place name, nature name
- ☐ **Stella** — Latin — star

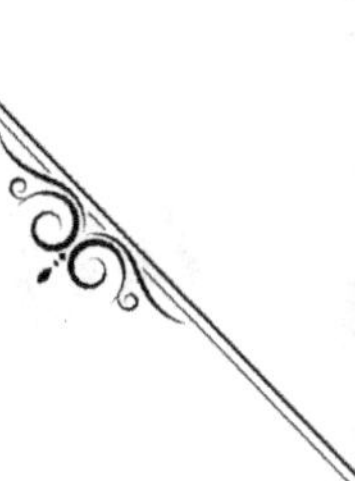

<u>Uncommon</u>

☐ **Aster** — English from Greek — star

☐ **Arcturus** — Greek — guardian of the bear, star name

☐ **Celestial** — Latin — of the heavens, planets or stars

☐ **Galileo** — Italian — from Galilee

☐ **Helia** — Greek — sun

☐ **Kepler** — surname German — mathematician and astronomer

☐ **Mercury** — Latin Roman — messenger/god of trade/planet name

☐ **Sagan** — Latin — wise, knowing, surname of astronomer

☐ **Sirius** — Latin from Greek — glowing, burning

☐ **Soleil** — French — sun

AUTUMN

Popular

☐ **Adam**   Hebrew   son of the red earth

☐ **Amber**   English   word name, color name

☐ **Autumn**   Latin   season name

☐ **Blaze**   Latin   fire, flame

☐ **Hunter**   English   one who hunts

☐ **October**   Latin   month name

☐ **Octavia**   Latin   eighth

☐ **Paisley**   Scottish   church, cemetery

☐ **Rory**   Irish   red king

☐ **Rust**   Old English   the color red

<u>Uncommon</u>

☐	**Acer**	Latin	maple
☐	**Crispin**	Latin	curly-haired
☐	**Dagan**	Hebrew	corn, grain
☐	**Golden**	Old English	gold
☐	**Harvest**	English	process of gathering crops
☐	**Jora**	Hebrew	autumn rain
☐	**Libra**	Greek	scales, balance
☐	**November**	Latin	ninth month
☐	**Radley**	English	red meadow
☐	**Wheatley**	English surname	surname from the wheat meadow

BEGINNINGS

Popular

☐ **Abel**	Hebrew	breath
☐ **Antonella**	Italian	firstborn
☐ **Aurora**	Latin	dawn
☐ **Dawn**	English	dawn, sunrise
☐ **January**	English	from the Roman god Janus
☐ **Genesis**	Greek	origin
☐ **Kady**	Irish	first
☐ **Kia**	African	season's beginning
☐ **Neon**	Greek	new
☐ **Phoenix**	Greek	dark red

Uncommon

☐	**Altan**	Turkish	red dawn
☐	**Arata**	Japanese	new, fresh
☐	**Dagny**	Scandinavian	new day
☐	**Fresco**	Italian	fresh
☐	**Inizio**	Italian	beginning
☐	**Neoma**	Greek	new moon
☐	**Renee**	French from Lat.	reborn
☐	**Tan**	Vietnamese	new
☐	**Zera**	Hebrew	seeds, beginning
☐	**Zoran**	Slavic	dawn, daybreak

BIBLICAL

Popular

☐	**Aaron**	Hebrew	high mountain, exalted, enlightened
☐	**Abraham**	Hebrew	father of multitudes
☐	**Deborah**	Hebrew	bee
☐	**Ezra**	Hebrew	help
☐	**Isaiah**	Hebrew	salvation of the Lord
☐	**Jonah**	Hebrew	dove
☐	**Joseph**	Hebrew	God will add
☐	**Leah**	Hebrew	weary
☐	**Levi**	Hebrew	joined in harmony, attached
☐	**Rachel**	Hebrew	ewe

<u>Uncommon</u>

☐ **Barnabas** — Aramaic — son of consolation

☐ **Cornelius** — Latin — horn

☐ **Damaris** — Greek — dominant woman

☐ **Ephron** — Hebrew — fawn-like

☐ **Gilead** — Hebrew — a camel hump

☐ **Jericho** — Arabic — city of the moon

☐ **Magdalena** — Greek — from Magdala

☐ **Shifra** — Hebrew — beautiful, good

☐ **Talitha** — Aramaic — little girl

☐ **Zipporah** — Hebrew — bird

BIRDS

Popular

☐	**Corbin**	Latin	crow
☐	**Dove**	Old English	dove, a bird
☐	**Falcon**	Eng. From French	dove, a bird
☐	**Gavin**	Celtic	white hawk
☐	**Hawk**	Old English	hawk, a bird
☐	**Lark**	English	songbird
☐	**Raven**	Old Norse/English	raven bird
☐	**Robin**	English	bright fame
☐	**Starling**	English	a bird
☐	**Wren**	English	small bird

Uncommon

☐	**Branwen**	Celtic	blessed raven
☐	**Canary**	English	small bird
☐	**Finch**	Old English	songbird
☐	**Halcyon**	Greek	kingfisher bird
☐	**Ingram**	German	angel-raven
☐	**Kestrel**	English	small colorful falcon
☐	**Lonan**	Irish	blackbird
☐	**Merla**	French	blackbird
☐	**Rooster**	English	roosting bird
☐	**Sparrow**	Old English	small bird

BLACK HISTORY

<u>Popular</u>

☐	**Audra**	English	noble strength
☐	**Booker**	English	scribe
☐	**Coretta**	English	maiden
☐	**Denzel**	Cornish	from the high stronghold
☐	**Ella**	German, English	all, completely, fairy maiden
☐	**Harriet**	English	estate ruler
☐	**Jada**	Spanish	jade
☐	**Martin**	Latin	warlike
☐	**Rosa**	Spanish, Italian	rose, a flower
☐	**Shirley**	English	bright meadow

Uncommon

- ☐ **Althea**   Greek   with healing power

- ☐ **Ida**   German   industrious one

- ☐ **Idris**   Welsh   lord

- ☐ **Langston**   English   tall man's town

- ☐ **Muhammad**   Arabic   praiseworthy

- ☐ **Robinson**   English   son of Robin

- ☐ **Tarana**   Hindi   born during the day

- ☐ **Thurgood**   Puritan   virtue name

- ☐ **Whitney**   English surname   white island

- ☐ **Zora**   Slavic   dawn

CITIES

Popular

☐	**Austin**	English	great, magnificent
☐	**Boston**	English	town by the woods
☐	**Dallas**	Scottish	from the meadow dwelling
☐	**Calgary**	Scottish	pasture by the bay
☐	**Denver**	English, French	green river, from Anvers
☐	**London**	Latin	from the great river, fortress of the moon
☐	**Orlando**	Italian	famous throughout the land
☐	**Paris**	Greek	from Paris, France
☐	**Rio**	Spanish	river
☐	**Vienna**	Latin	city in Austria

Uncommon

☐	**Aberdeen**	Scottish	at the mouth of Don
☐	**Dover**	Celtic	the waters
☐	**Galway**	Gaelic	stranger, foreigner
☐	**Geneva**	French	juniper tree
☐	**Lourdes**	Basque	craggy slope
☐	**Reno**	Spanish	born again
☐	**Vail**	English	dweller in the valley
☐	**Verona**	Italian	true image
☐	**York**	English	from the yew estate
☐	**Zaria**	Slavic or Arabic	princess, blooming flower, or rose

COLORS

Popular

☐	**Bleu**	French	blue
☐	**Crimson**	English	rich, deep red
☐	**Ebony**	English	dark black wood
☐	**Gray**	English	gray-haired
☐	**Indigo**	Greek	blue dye from India
☐	**Mauve**	French	purplish, violet, mallow plant
☐	**Navy**	English	dark blue, a fleet of ships
☐	**Scarlet**	English	scarlet, red
☐	**Sienna**	Italian	orange-red, from Siena
☐	**Violet**	Latin	purple

Uncommon

☐	**Azul**	Spanish	blue
☐	**Chartreuse**	French	yellow-green, charterhouse
☐	**Cyan**	English	greenish-blue
☐	**Ecru**	French	beige, raw, unbleached
☐	**Magenta**	Italian	deep pink
☐	**Mazarine**	French	dark blue
☐	**Roux**	French	reddish brown, russet
☐	**Russet**	Old English	reddish
☐	**Tawny**	English	golden brown
☐	**Umber**	French	brown, shade

COUNTRY WESTERN

Popular

☐	**Blake**	English	fair-haired or dark
☐	**Chase**	French	to hunt
☐	**Faye**	English or French	fairy
☐	**Georgia**	English	farmer
☐	**Hadley**	English	heather field
☐	**Hank**	German	estate ruler
☐	**Mason**	English	worker in stone
☐	**Nolan**	Irish	champion
☐	**Peyton**	English	fighting-man's estate
☐	**Preston**	English	priest's estate

<u>Uncommon</u>

☐	**Dusty**	Norse	brave warrior or Thor's stone
☐	**Earl**	English	nobleman
☐	**Easton**	English	east facing place
☐	**Kinsey**	English	king's victory
☐	**Lainey**	French	bright, shining light
☐	**Mabel**	Latin	lovable
☐	**Ryker**	German	rich
☐	**Tabitha**	Aramaic	gazelle
☐	**Walker**	English	fuller of cloth
☐	**Zeke**	Hebrew	God strengthens

ELEGANT

Popular

- [ ] **Adelaide** German noble, nobility
- [ ] **Caroline** French free man
- [ ] **Francesca** Italian, Latin from France, free
- [ ] **Gregory** Greek vigilant, watchful
- [ ] **Henrietta** English ruler of the home
- [ ] **Leonardo** Italian, Spanish brave as a lion
- [ ] **Maximilian** Latin greatest
- [ ] **Montgomery** English from the hill of the powerful man
- [ ] **Remington** English place on a riverbank
- [ ] **Tatiana** Russian unknown

<u>Uncommon</u>

☐	**Arabella**	Latin	yielding to prayer
☐	**Bartholomew**	Aramaic	son of the furrow
☐	**Caledonia**	Latin	hard or rocky land
☐	**Deveraux**	French	from Evreux, France
☐	**Euphemia**	Greek	well-spoken
☐	**Ferdinand**	German	bold voyager
☐	**Fiorella**	Italian	little flower
☐	**Kingston**	English	king's town
☐	**Ottilie**	German, French	prosperous in battle, rich, wealthy
☐	**Willoughby**	English	farm near the willows

ENGLISH

Popular

☐ **Addison** English son of Adam

☐ **Avery** English ruler of elves

☐ **Edwin** English rich or wealthy friend

☐ **Harper** English harp player

☐ **Holmes** English from islands in the river

☐ **Jameson** English son of James

☐ **Kingsley** English king's meadow

☐ **Lucy** English light

☐ **Paige** English page to a lord

☐ **Taylor** English tailor

<u>Uncommon</u>

☐	**Ashby**	English	by the ash tree
☐	**Boswell**	English	well near the woods
☐	**Elfrida**	English	elf power
☐	**Gardner**	English	keeper of the garden
☐	**Holt**	English	a small wood
☐	**Mosley**	English	peat bog, mouse clearing
☐	**Oswald**	English	divine power
☐	**Radcliff**	English	red cliff
☐	**Seldon**	English	from the house on the hill
☐	**Whitford**	English	from the white ford

FAIRY TALES

Popular

☐	**Ariel**	Hebrew	lion of God
☐	**Belle**	French	beautiful
☐	**Elsa**	German	pledged to God
☐	**Eric**	Old Norse	eternal ruler
☐	**Flynn**	Irish	son of the red-haired one
☐	**Gretel**	German	pearl
☐	**Jack**	English	God is gracious
☐	**Philip**	Greek	lover of horses
☐	**Sebastian**	Latin from Greek	Latin from Greek person from Sebastia, venerable
☐	**Wendy**	English	friend, family, wanderer

<u>Uncommon</u>

☐	**Castle**	English	fort
☐	**Eudora**	Greek	generous gift
☐	**Fable**	English	story with a moral or lesson
☐	**Figaro**	French	barber
☐	**Gaston**	French	foreigner, guest
☐	**Locket**	French	necklace, keepsake
☐	**Nala**	African	queen, lion, successful
☐	**Naveen**	Hindi	new
☐	**Pixie**	Swedish, Cornish	Swedish, Cornish fairy
☐	**Rapunzel**	German	rampion, lamb's lettuce

FLOWERS

Popular

☐	**Blossom**	English	to bloom
☐	**Daisy**	English	day's eye
☐	**Florent**	French	flowering
☐	**Heather**	English	evergreen flowering plant
☐	**Lavender**	English	purple flower
☐	**Lily**	Latin	pure
☐	**Magnolia**	French	Magnol's flower
☐	**Marigold**	English	golden flower
☐	**Posey**	English	a bunch of flowers
☐	**Rose**	Latin	rose, a flower

Uncommon

☐ **Acacia**	Greek	thorny
☐ **Azalea**	Greek	dry
☐ **Blodwyn**	Welsh	white flower
☐ **Calla**	Greek	beautiful
☐ **Daffodil**	English	yellow flower
☐ **Edelweiss**	German	noble white
☐ **Petal**	Greek	leaf
☐ **Ren**	Japanese	water lily, lotus
☐ **Wisteria**	English	Wister's flower
☐ **Zinnia**	German	Zinn's flower

FOOD

Popular

☐	**Almond**	English, German	almond, noble strength
☐	**Apple**	English	the apple fruit
☐	**Brandy**	Dutch	burnt wine
☐	**Berry**	Old English	fortified place, small fruit
☐	**Clementine**	French, Latin	mild, merciful
☐	**Fraser**	Scottish	strawberry
☐	**Lollie**	French	free man, diminutive of Charlotte
☐	**Olive**	English	olive tree
☐	**Sherry**	French	beloved
☐	**Taffy**	Welsh	beloved friend

<u>Uncommon</u>

☐	**Ambrosia**	Greek, Latin	immortal
☐	**Avalon**	Celtic	island of apples
☐	**Cerise**	French	cherry
☐	**Cocoa**	Spanish	powdered chocolate
☐	**Dolce**	Italian	sweet
☐	**Kale**	Hawaiian	free man
☐	**Linnea**	Swedish	lime tree, twinflower
☐	**Nori**	Japanese	seaweed or doctrine
☐	**Shallot**	French from Latin	bulbous perennial onion
☐	**Quince**	Latin	apple-like fruit

FRENCH

<u>Popular</u>

☐	**Adelyn**	French	noble, nobility
☐	**Antoinette**	French	priceless one, highly praiseworthy
☐	**Celine**	French from Latin	heavenly
☐	**Charlotte**	French	free man
☐	**Eloise**	French	healthy, wide
☐	**Gabrielle**	French	God is my strength
☐	**Jolie**	French	pretty
☐	**Marc**	French	warlike, from the god mars
☐	**Remy**	French from Latin	oarsman
☐	**Warren**	French, English	park keeper

<u>Uncommon</u>

☐	**Arlette**	French	noble, honor
☐	**Aubin**	French	white, blond
☐	**Bijou**	French	jewel
☐	**Cadeau**	French	gift
☐	**Delano**	French	from the forest of nut trees
☐	**Gage**	French	oath, pledge
☐	**Landry**	French, English	ruler
☐	**Odette**	French from German	wealthy
☐	**Parnell**	French	little Peter
☐	**Ranger**	French	forest guardian

GEMSTONES

<u>Popular</u>

☐ **Amethyst**   Greek   not intoxicated

☐ **Crystal**   Latin, Greek   clear glass, ice

☐ **Emerald**   Persian, English   green gemstone

☐ **Gold**   Old English   gold

☐ **Jade**   Spanish, English   stone of the side, gemstone

☐ **Jewel**   English   precious stone

☐ **Opal**   Sanskrit   jewel, precious stone

☐ **Pearl**   Latin   pearl

☐ **Ruby**   Latin   deep red precious stone

☐ **Sapphire**   Latin, Greek   blue

Uncommon

☐	**Agate**	French	semi-precious stone
☐	**Beryl**	Greek	light green semi-precious gemstone
☐	**Garnet**	English	dark red gemstone named for pomegranate
☐	**Giada**	Italian	jade
☐	**Quartz**	German	hard crystalline mineral
☐	**Onyx**	Latin	black gemstone
☐	**Peridot**	Arabic, French	green gemstone
☐	**Silver**	English	white precious metal
☐	**Topaz**	Greek, Latin	golden gem
☐	**Ula**	Celtic	gem of the sea

GRACE

<u>Popular</u>

☐	**Evan**	Welsh	the Lord is gracious
☐	**Gianna**	Italian	God is gracious
☐	**Hans**	German, Scand.	God is gracious
☐	**Ian**	Scottish	the Lord is gracious
☐	**Jane**	English	God is gracious
☐	**Jean**	French	God is gracious
☐	**John**	Hebrew	God is gracious
☐	**Sean**	Irish	God is gracious
☐	**Sheena**	Irish	God is gracious
☐	**Zane**	Hebrew	God is gracious

<u>Uncommon</u>

☐ **Carissa**   Greek   grace, beloved

☐ **Eoin**   Irish   God is gracious

☐ **Janisa**   Hebrew   God is gracious

☐ **Kalasia**   Tongan   Polynesian graceful woman

☐ **Jonesy**   English   God is gracious

☐ **Ninette**   French   grace

☐ **Lienna**   Chinese   beauty and grace of a lotus flower

☐ **Ohanna**   Armenian   God's gracious gift

☐ **Vanya**   Slavic   gracious gift of God

☐ **Yannick**   Hebrew or French   God is gracious

GREEK

<u>Popular</u>

☐ **Alexander** Greek   defender of the people

☐ **Callista** Greek   most beautiful

☐ **Damien** Greek   to tame, subdue

☐ **Judas** Greek   praised

☐ **Phoebe** Greek   radiant, shining one

☐ **Peter** Greek   rock

☐ **Sophia** Greek   wisdom

☐ **Stephanie** Greek   garland, crown

☐ **Theodore** Greek   gift of God

☐ **Zoe** Greek   life

<u>Uncommon</u>

☐	**Aristotle**	Greek	the best of all, superior
☐	**Atticus**	Greek	from Attica
☐	**Cosima**	Greek	order, beauty
☐	**Cyril**	Greek	lordly
☐	**Daphne**	Greek	laurel tree, bay tree
☐	**Demetrius**	Greek	follower of Demeter, of the earth
☐	**Evanthe**	Greek	fair flower, good flower
☐	**Medora**	Greek	mother's gift
☐	**Rhea**	Greek	flowing stream
☐	**Stavros**	Greek	cross

GREEK MYTHOLOGY

<u>Popular</u>

☐	**Apollo**	Greek	destroyer, god of poetry and music
☐	**Artemis**	Greek	goddess of hunting, butcher
☐	**Athena**	Greek	goddess of wisdom/war, from Athens
☐	**Demeter**	Greek	goddess of agriculture, earth mother
☐	**Griffin**	Welsh	eagle/lion creature, strong lord
☐	**Hera**	Greek	goddess of marriage/childbirth
☐	**Homer**	Greek	ancient Greek author, security, pledge
☐	**Icarus**	Greek	tragic figure of pride, follower
☐	**Triton**	Aramaic	god of the sea, merman
☐	**Zeus**	Greek	god of sky, ruler of all gods

<u>Uncommon</u>

☐ **Argo**   Greek   ship that Jason sailed, lazy, slothful

☐ **Cadmus**   Greek   first king of Thebes, one who excels

☐ **Calliope**   Greek   muse of epic poetry, beautiful-voiced

☐ **Dionysus**   Greek   god of wine, god of Nysa

☐ **Eros**   Greek   god of love, desire

☐ **Hector**   Greek   Trojan prince and warrior, holding fast

☐ **Pallas**   Greek   god of battle/warcraft, wisdom

☐ **Poseidon**   Greek   god of the sea/storms

☐ **Selene**   Greek   goddess of the moon

☐ **Theseus**   Greek   Athenian hero/demi-god, to set

HAPPY

Popular

☐	**Abigail**	Hebrew	brings joy, my father's joy
☐	**Asher**	Hebrew	fortunate, blessed, happy one
☐	**Beatrice**	Latin	she who brings happiness, blessed, voyager
☐	**Blythe**	English	happy, carefree, cheerful
☐	**Felicity**	Latin	good fortune, happy
☐	**Felix**	Latin	happy, fortunate
☐	**Gwyneth**	Welsh	blessed, happy
☐	**Isaac**	Hebrew	one who laughs
☐	**Naomi**	Hebrew	pleasantness, gentle, beautiful
☐	**Tate**	English from Norse	cheerful

<u>Uncommon</u>

☐	**Chara**	Greek	joy, happiness
☐	**Fane**	English	happy, joyous
☐	**Keiko**	Japanese	happy child
☐	**Leta**	Latin	glad, joyful
☐	**Onni**	Finnish	happiness, luck
☐	**Preeda**	Thai	joyful
☐	**Revel**	English	rejoice
☐	**Seeley**	French, English	blessed, happy
☐	**Thirza**	Hebrew	delightful, pleasant, harvest
☐	**Zorion**	Basque	happiness

HEBREW

<u>Popular</u>

☐	**Benjamin**	Hebrew	son of the right hand
☐	**Danielle**	Hebrew	God is my judge
☐	**Delilah**	Hebrew, Arabic	delicate
☐	**Eden**	Hebrew	place of pleasure, delight
☐	**Elizabeth**	Hebrew	God is my oath
☐	**Kayla**	Hebrew, American	laurel, crown, God-like, pure
☐	**Micah**	Hebrew	Who is like God
☐	**Noah**	Hebrew	rest, repose
☐	**Sara**	Hebrew	princess
☐	**Zachary**	Hebrew	God remembers

<u>Uncommon</u>

☐ **Amari** Hebrew eternal, immortal

☐ **Avi** Hebrew father

☐ **Bethel** Hebrew house of God

☐ **Eben** Hebrew stone of help

☐ **Maven** Hebrew one who understands

☐ **Orli** Hebrew my light

☐ **Shira** Hebrew poetry, singing

☐ **Solomon** Hebrew peaceful one

☐ **Uziel** Hebrew God is my power

☐ **Zimri** Hebrew my music, my praise

INVENTED

Popular

- ☐ **Briley** — Irish — descendant of Roghallach

- ☐ **Cason** — Modern — unknown

- ☐ **Evolet** — Modern — the promise of life, movie character

- ☐ **Jaxon** — English — son of Jack

- ☐ **Jovie** — American — character from movie *Elf*

- ☐ **Kayden** — American — fighter

- ☐ **Maverick** — American — independent, non-conformist

- ☐ **Maxon** — Latin — greatest

- ☐ **Rocco** — Italian — rest, repose

- ☐ **Tinley** — Old English — hedge, fence, or clearing

<u>Uncommon</u>

☐	**Anakin**	American	character in *Star Wars*
☐	**Daenerys**	Modern	character in *Game of Thrones*
☐	**Elphaba**	American	Gregory Maguire's novel *Wicked*
☐	**Genova**	American	new wave
☐	**Irelyn**	Modern	variation of Ireland
☐	**Khaleesi**	Modern	character in *Game of Thrones*
☐	**Lathan**	English	barn or farm by the water
☐	**Theoden**	Literature	king
☐	**Todrick**	American	mash-up of two names
☐	**Vanellope**	American	Disney character in *Wreck-It Ralph*

IRISH

<u>Popular</u>

☐	**Brigid**	Irish	exalted one, strength, lofty
☐	**Conor**	Irish	lover of hounds
☐	**Darren**	Irish	little great one
☐	**Finley**	Irish	fair-haired hero
☐	**Kennedy**	Irish	misshapen head, helmeted head
☐	**Liam**	Irish	resolute protection
☐	**Maeve**	Irish	she who intoxicates
☐	**Quinn**	Irish	descendent of Conn
☐	**Riley**	Irish	from the rye clearing, courageous/valiant
☐	**Saoirse**	Irish	freedom

<u>Uncommon</u>

☐	**Aoife**	Irish	beautiful, radiant
☐	**Aisling**	Irish	dream, vision
☐	**Breccan**	Irish	freckled, speckled
☐	**Cormac**	Irish	son of the charioteer
☐	**Muriel**	Irish	sea bright
☐	**Niamh**	Irish	bright
☐	**Oisin**	Irish	little deer
☐	**Padraig**	Irish	patrician, noble
☐	**Tadhg**	Irish	poet, philosopher
☐	**Tully**	Irish	Peaceful, hill

LATIN

Popular

☐ **Anthony** — Latin — priceless one, from Antium

☐ **Benedict** — Latin — blessed

☐ **Cecelia** — Latin — blind

☐ **Julian** — Latin, English — youthful, sky father

☐ **Paul** — Latin — humble, small

☐ **Priscilla** — Latin — ancient

☐ **Roman** — Latin — citizen of Rome

☐ **Serena** — Latin — tranquil, serene

☐ **Silas** — Latin, English — wood, forest

☐ **Victoria** — Latin — victory, winner, conqueror

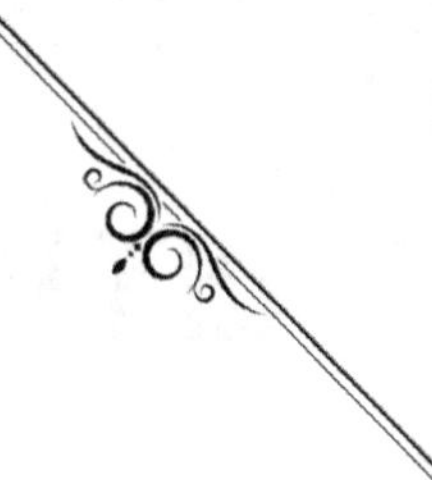

<u>Uncommon</u>

☐ **Aurelius**   Latin   the golden one

☐ **Carmine**   Latin   song

☐ **Gemini**   Latin   twins

☐ **Lawrence**   Latin   from Laurentium

☐ **Lux**   Latin   light

☐ **Marcella**   Latin   warlike

☐ **Pomona**   Latin   fruit tree

☐ **Quintin**   Latin   fifth

☐ **Sylvia**   Latin   from the forest

☐ **Una**   Latin   lamb, one

LITERARY

Popular

☐	**Austen**	English	great, magnificent
☐	**Beckett**	English	bee hive or dweller by the brook
☐	**Byron**	English	barn for cows
☐	**Darcy**	French	dark one or from Arcy
☐	**Emily**	Latin	rival
☐	**Holden**	English	hollow valley
☐	**Joyce**	Latin, English	merry, joyous or little lord
☐	**Meg**	English from Greek	pearl
☐	**Shelley**	English	clearing on a bank
☐	**Wilbur**	German, English	resolute, brilliant, will fortress

<u>Uncommon</u>

☐	**Alcott**	English	dweller at the old cottage
☐	**Bronte**	Greek	thunder
☐	**Ernest**	English	serious, resolute
☐	**Fitzgerald**	Irish, Scottish	beson of Gerald
☐	**Gatsby**	German	from Gaddesby
☐	**Hermione**	Greek	messenger
☐	**Lowry**	Scottish	from Laurentum
☐	**Poe**	English	peacock
☐	**Salinger**	French, Norman	Saint Leger, peace
☐	**Tennyson**	English	son of Dennis

LOVE

Popular

☐	**Amanda**	Latin	she who must be loved
☐	**Aziz**	Arabic	beloved and powerful
☐	**Cher**	French	dear one, darling, beloved
☐	**Darlene**	Old English	darling
☐	**David**	Hebrew	beloved
☐	**Esme**	French	loved, admired
☐	**Lennon**	Irish	lover, dear one
☐	**Lev**	Hebrew	heart
☐	**Milena**	Czech	pleasant, love, dear, gracious
☐	**Priya**	Sanskrit	beloved

<u>Uncommon</u>

☐ **Adelpha**	Greek	beloved sister
☐ **Ahava**	Hebrew	love
☐ **Caradoc**	Welsh	amiable, beloved
☐ **Carys**	Welsh	to love
☐ **Corwin**	Gaelic, English	heart's friend
☐ **Femi**	African	love me
☐ **Frigg**	Old Norse	beloved
☐ **Luba**	Slavic	love, dear
☐ **Obi**	Nigerian	heart
☐ **Suki**	Japanese	beloved

MAGICAL

Popular

☐	**Ambrose**	Latin	immortal
☐	**Boone**	English, French	blessing, lucky, good
☐	**Draco**	Greek from Latin	dragon
☐	**Enid**	Welsh	spirit, life
☐	**Gandalf**	Norse	wand elf
☐	**Lilith**	Assyrian	ghost, night monster
☐	**Mage**	Latin	learned magician
☐	**Regin**	Old Norse	mythical blacksmith, ruler's advisor
☐	**Salem**	Hebrew, Arabic	peaceful, safe
☐	**Zelda**	German	gray fighting maid

<u>Uncommon</u>

☐	**Alvin**	English	friend of the elves
☐	**Aislinn**	Irish	dream
☐	**Belladonna**	English from Italian	deadly nightshade, beautiful lady
☐	**Charm**	English	lucky token
☐	**Cybele**	Greek	the mother of all gods
☐	**Maldue**	Arthurian	wizard
☐	**Nixie**	German	water nymph
☐	**Pegasus**	Greek	from a water spring
☐	**Reverie**	French	daydream
☐	**Rune**	Scandinavian	secret

MUSICAL

Popular

	Name	Origin	Meaning
☐	**Aria**	Italian and Hebrew	air, song or melody, and lion
☐	**Brahms**	German, Hebrew	father of multitudes
☐	**Cadence**	Latin	rhythm, beat
☐	**Drummer**	English	one who drums
☐	**Harmony**	Greek	unity or concord
☐	**Handel**	German	trade or commerce
☐	**Lyra**	Greek, Latin	lyre, harp
☐	**Melody**	Greek	music or song
☐	**Mozart**	German	bog, marsh
☐	**Octave**	French	eighth

Uncommon

☐	**Cantata**	Italian	musical composition with vocal elements
☐	**Evensong**	English	evening service, vespers
☐	**Gershwin**	Hebrew	related to music or melody
☐	**Jazz**	English	style of music
☐	**Rhapsody**	French	ecstatic expression of feeling
☐	**Serenade**	Latin	one who sings a song of love
☐	**Soprano**	Italian	higher situated above
☐	**Symphony**	Greek	musical piece
☐	**Tempo**	Italian	time
☐	**Vivaldi**	Italian, Latin	life

NATURE

Popular

☐ **Acker**	English or German	meadow of oak trees, field
☐ **Breeze**	English	a light gentle wind
☐ **Clay**	English	clay worker, sticky earth
☐ **Ember**	English, French	spark, burning low
☐ **Gaia**	Greek	earth goddess
☐ **Meadow**	English	field of grass, vegetation
☐ **Moon**	English	from the moon
☐ **Savannah**	Spanish	flat, tropical grassland
☐ **Slate**	English	gray-green rock
☐ **Terra**	Latin	earth

<u>Uncommon</u>

☐ **Aloe**	English, Greek	aloe, resin
☐ **Bramble**	English	blackberry shrub
☐ **Canyon**	Spanish	a large ravine, footpath
☐ **Clover**	English	meadow flower
☐ **Granite**	Latin	hard, igneous rock
☐ **Hawthorne**	English	lives where hawthorn hedges grow
☐ **Moss**	English	born of a god
☐ **Parks**	Chinese, English	cypress tree, at the park
☐ **Roscoe**	Norse	deer forest
☐ **Thistle**	English	to prick

NICKNAMES

Popular

☐	**Ash**	English	ash tree
☐	**Cal**	Latin	bald, hairless
☐	**Dottie**	English	gift of God
☐	**Drew**	Greek	strong and manly
☐	**Eli**	Hebrew	ascended, uplifted, high
☐	**Gwen**	Welsh	white, holy
☐	**Joey**	English	God will increase
☐	**Lee**	English	pasture, meadow, field
☐	**Mia**	varied	mine or bitter
☐	**Sam**	Hebrew	told by God

<u>Uncommon</u>

☐ **Ace**   Latin   one, unity

☐ **Desi**   French or Spanish   desired

☐ **Fifi**   French   Jehovah increases

☐ **Link**   English   town by the pool

☐ **Lettie**   English, Latin   joy, gladness

☐ **Mack**   Scottish, Irish   son of

☐ **Mo**   varied   dark-skinned, savior

☐ **Pippa**   English   lover of horses

☐ **Stan**   English   from the stony field

☐ **Wyn**   Welsh   fair, blessed

NORDIC

Popular

☐ **Anders**   Scandinavian   strong and manly

☐ **Axel**   Scandinavian   father of peace

☐ **Bjorn**   Scandinavian   bear

☐ **Freya**   Old Norse   a noble woman

☐ **Gunnar**   Scandinavian   bold warrior

☐ **Ingrid**   Old Norse   air, Ing is beautiful

☐ **Lars**   Scandinavian   crowned with laurel, from Laurentum

☐ **Liv**   Old Norse   life

☐ **Nils**   Scandinavian   people of victory

☐ **Odin**   Old Norse   god of frenzy, poetic fury

Uncommon

☐ **Asgard**	Old Norse	God's courtyard
☐ **Astrid**	Scandinavian	divinely beautiful
☐ **Baldur**	Old Norse	prince
☐ **Birger**	Old Norse	to help, to save, to rescue
☐ **Embla**	Old Norse	elm
☐ **Mimir**	Old Norse	he who remembers, the wise one
☐ **Sanna**	Scandinavian	lily
☐ **Signy**	Scandinavian	new victory
☐ **Tove**	Scandinavian	beautiful
☐ **Viggo**	Old Norse	battle, fight

OCCUPATIONS

Popular

☐	**Archer**	English	bowman
☐	**Becker**	German	baker
☐	**Carter**	English	driver of a cart
☐	**Cooper**	Hebrew	barrel maker
☐	**Deacon**	Greek	messenger, servant
☐	**Hooper**	English	hoop maker
☐	**Parker**	English	park keeper
☐	**Porter**	English, French	doorkeeper
☐	**Sawyer**	English	woodcutter
☐	**Spencer**	English	butler, steward

<u>Uncommon</u>

☐ **Bayless** French bailiff

☐ **Carden** English wool carder

☐ **Decker** German roofer

☐ **Draper** English cloth merchant

☐ **Foster** English forester

☐ **Granger** English, French worker of the granary, farmer

☐ **Jagger** English carter, peddler

☐ **Roper** English rope maker

☐ **Wagner** German wagon maker

☐ **Whistler** English piper

OLD HOLLYWOOD

<u>Popular</u>

☐ **Audrey**   English   noble strength

☐ **Charlie**   English, French   free man

☐ **Clark**   English   scribe, clerk

☐ **Dean**   English   from the valley, church official

☐ **Fred**   English, German   peaceful ruler

☐ **Greta**   German   pearl

☐ **Joan**   Hebrew   God is gracious

☐ **Kelly**   Irish   bright-headed, warrior

☐ **Marilyn**   English combo   bitter, drop of the sea, beloved + lake

☐ **Stewart**   Scottish   steward

Uncommon

	Name	Origin	Meaning
☐	**Brando**	Italian	sword or fiery torch
☐	**Claudette**	French	lame, enclosure
☐	**Doris**	Greek	gift of the ocean
☐	**Eartha**	English	earth
☐	**Garland**	English, French	land of the spear, wreath, prize
☐	**Humphrey**	English, German	peaceful warrior
☐	**Kirk**	Norse	church
☐	**Mickey**	Hebrew	who is like God
☐	**Rita**	Spanish	pearl
☐	**Sidney**	French	Saint Denis

PERSIAN

Popular

☐	**Aleah**	Persian, Arabic	high, exalted, God's being
☐	**Cyrus**	Persian	sun
☐	**Eskander**	Persian, Arabic	defender of men
☐	**Esther**	Persian	star
☐	**Jasmine**	Persian	gift from God
☐	**Jasper**	Persian	bringer of treasure
☐	**Kayvan**	Persian, Iranian	Saturn, world, universe
☐	**Leila**	Persian, Arabic	night
☐	**Rosetta**	Persian, Italian	splendid, little rose
☐	**Roxanne**	Persian	dawn

<u>Uncommon</u>

☐	**Armani**	Persian, Italian	soldier or wish, hope
☐	**Darius**	Persian, Greek, Lat.	possessing goodness
☐	**Farhad**	Persian	gained, earned, happiness
☐	**Nariman**	Persian	faith and brightness
☐	**Parisa**	Persian	fairy-like
☐	**Ramin**	Persian	rescuer from hunger and pain
☐	**Reza**	Persian, Arabic	contentment, satisfaction
☐	**Shirin**	Persian	charming, sweet
☐	**Vashti**	Persian	lovely, beautiful
☐	**Zarina**	Persian	golden

RAINBOW BABIES

Popular

☐	**Bennett**	English from Latin	blessed
☐	**Clarabelle**	Latin	bright, beautiful
☐	**Eliana**	Hebrew	God has answered
☐	**Evangeline**	Greek	bearer of good news
☐	**Iris**	Greek	rainbow
☐	**Jesse**	Hebrew	gift
☐	**Joanna**	English	God is gracious
☐	**Kiran**	Sanskrit	sunbeam, ray of light
☐	**Samuel**	Hebrew	God has heard, name of God
☐	**Vera**	Russian	faith

Uncommon

☐	**Adora**	Latin	adored
☐	**Araceli**	Spanish	altar of the sky
☐	**Enfys**	Welsh	rainbow
☐	**Godiva**	English	God's gift
☐	**Iridiana**	Greek	rainbow
☐	**Keyne**	Cornish	man of the eastern sky
☐	**Liora**	Hebrew	my light
☐	**Neven**	Irish, Latin	holy, sacred
☐	**Noelani**	Hawaiian	mist of heaven
☐	**Raphaela**	Hebrew	God has healed

ROMAN MYTHOLOGY

<u>Popular</u>

☐	**Diana**	Greek, Latin	divine, goddess of animals and hunting
☐	**Flora**	Latin	flower, goddess of flowers
☐	**Janus**	Latin	God of beginnings, doorway
☐	**Juno**	Latin	queen of heaven, goddess of childbirth
☐	**Jupiter**	Latin	god of the sky, godfather
☐	**Maia**	Greek	mother, mother of Hermes
☐	**Neptune**	Latin	god of the sea
☐	**Pluto**	Latin	god of the underworld, rich
☐	**Silvia**	Latin	from the woods, goddess of the forest
☐	**Venus**	Latin	goddess of love and beauty

<u>Uncommon</u>

☐	**Bellona**	Latin	goddess of war
☐	**Ceres**	Latin	goddess of the harvest
☐	**Cupid**	Latin	desire, god of love
☐	**Liber**	Latin	free, god of wine, male fertility
☐	**Lucina**	Latin	grove or light, goddess of childbirth
☐	**Minerva**	Latin	of the mind, intellect, goddess of arts and war
☐	**Nona**	Latin	ninth, spinner of the thread of life
☐	**Remus**	Latin	twin of Romulus, founded Rome
☐	**Tiberius**	Latin	of the Tiber river, Roman emperor
☐	**Vesta**	Latin	pure, goddess of domestic life

SCOTTISH

<u>Popular</u>

☐	**Brody**	Scottish	broad eye or broad island
☐	**Campbell**	Scottish	crooked mouth
☐	**Douglas**	Scottish	black water
☐	**Fiona**	Scottish	white, fair
☐	**Graham**	Scottish	gravelly homestead
☐	**Hamish**	Scottish	supplanter
☐	**Lachlan**	Scottish	from the land of the lakes
☐	**Logan**	Scottish	small hollow
☐	**Malcolm**	Scottish	devotee of St. Colomba
☐	**McKenna**	Scottish, Irish	son of Kenneth

<u>Uncommon</u>

☐	**Ailsa**	Scottish from Norse	elf victory
☐	**Alisdair**	Scottish	defending men
☐	**Duncan**	Scottish	dark warrior
☐	**Greer**	Scottish	alert, watchful
☐	**Ewan**	Scottish	born of the yew tree
☐	**Fergus**	Scottish, Irish	man of force, strong
☐	**Innes**	Scottish	from the river island
☐	**Morag**	Scottish	great
☐	**Wallace**	Scottish, English	foreigner, stranger
☐	**Wylie**	Scottish	resolute protection

SHAKESPEARE

Popular

☐	**Bianca**	Italian	white
☐	**Cassius**	Latin	hollow, vain
☐	**Edgar**	English	wealthy spearman
☐	**Imogen**	Celtic	maiden
☐	**Juliet**	English from Latin	youthful or sky father
☐	**Miranda**	Latin	admirable, marvelous
☐	**Portia**	Latin	pig, hog, or doorway
☐	**Regan**	Irish	little king
☐	**Romeo**	Italian	from Rome, Roman
☐	**Rosalind**	German or Spanish	gentle horse or pretty rose

<u>Uncommon</u>

☐ **Benvolio** Italian good wisher

☐ **Cressida** Greek gold

☐ **Desdemona** Greek ill-fated

☐ **Hamlet** English, Danish village, home

☐ **Hermia** Greek messenger

☐ **Hippolyta** Greek releaser of horses

☐ **Lysander** Greek liberator

☐ **Montague** French pointy hill

☐ **Oberon** English noble, bearlike

☐ **Puck** unknown mischievous

SLAVIC

Popular

☐	**Anton**	Slavic or Greek	priceless or flower
☐	**Boris**	Slavic	to fight
☐	**Christo**	Slavic	one who carries Christ
☐	**Danica**	Slavic	morning star
☐	**Mila**	Slavic, Russian	gracious, dear
☐	**Nadia**	Slavic	hope
☐	**Oksana**	Slavic	praise be to God
☐	**Raina**	Slavic	queen
☐	**Stanislav**	Slavic	becoming glorious
☐	**Tiana**	Slavic	fairy queen

<u>Uncommon</u>

☐	**Alina**	Slavic	bright, beautiful
☐	**Baruska**	Slavic, Latin	foreign woman
☐	**Chessa**	Slavic	peaceful
☐	**Damek**	Slavic	earth
☐	**Elga**	Slavic	sacred
☐	**Jovan**	Slavic, Latin	jove-like, majestic
☐	**Lala**	Slavic	laurel
☐	**Tibor**	Slavic	of Tibur (Tivoli)
☐	**Ziven**	Slavic	vigorous, lively
☐	**Zorina**	Slavic	golden dawn

SPANISH

Popular

☐	**Arsenio**	Spanish from Greek	virile, strong
☐	**Carlos**	Spanish	free man
☐	**Cruz**	Spanish	cross
☐	**Diego**	Spanish	supplanter
☐	**Elena**	Spanish and others	bright, shining light
☐	**Isabel**	Spanish	pledged to God
☐	**Maritza**	Spanish	drop of the sea, bitter, beloved
☐	**Ricardo**	Spanish	dominant ruler
☐	**Salvador**	Spanish	savior
☐	**Sierra**	Spanish	mountain range, saw-toothed

Uncommon

☐ **Anacita**	Spanish from Latin	unconquerable
☐ **Brisa**	Spanish	breeze
☐ **Carmen**	Spanish, Hebrew	song, poetry, garden
☐ **Catalina**	Spanish	pure
☐ **Marisol**	Spanish	sea and sun
☐ **Mercedes**	Spanish	gracious gifts, benefits
☐ **Nelo**	Spanish	God is my judge
☐ **Paloma**	Spanish	dove
☐ **Santiago**	Spanish	St. James
☐ **Vasco**	Spanish	someone from the Basque region or crow

SPICES

Popular

- [ ] **Anise** — English — spice
- [ ] **Basil** — Greek — royal, kingly
- [ ] **Cayenne** — French — hot spice
- [ ] **Clove** — Latin — a nail
- [ ] **Ginger** — English — pure, chaste
- [ ] **Mint** — Latin — yielding to prayer
- [ ] **Pepper** — Sanskrit, English — berry
- [ ] **Rosemary** — Latin — dew of the sea
- [ ] **Saffron** — English — yellow flower
- [ ] **Sage** — Latin — wise and knowing

<u>Uncommon</u>

☐ **Bay**   Latin, English   berry, sea inlet

☐ **Caraway**   unclear   unclear

☐ **Cinnamon**   Greek   a spice

☐ **Coriander**   Greek   bed bug

☐ **Fennel**   Latin   little hay

☐ **Sesame**   English   resembling the flavorful seed

☐ **Tamarind**   Arabic   tree and spice name

☐ **Thyme**   Old French   herb of the mint family

☐ **Vanilla**   Spanish from Latin   little pod, sheath

☐ **Yarrow**   English   rough stream

SPRING

<u>Popular</u>

	Name	Language	Meaning
☐	**Afternoon**	English	afternoon
☐	**April**	Latin	to open
☐	**Birdie**	English	little bird
☐	**Eva**	Latin	life
☐	**Fern**	English	green plant
☐	**Leif**	Scandinavian	heir
☐	**May**	English	drop of the sea, bitter or beloved
☐	**June**	Latin	follower of Juno
☐	**Primrose**	English	first rose
☐	**Wells**	English	spring

<u>Uncommon</u>

☐ **Aviva**   Hebrew   springlike, fresh, dewy

☐ **Chloris**   Greek   pale green, goddess of spring and flowers

☐ **Fairweather**   English   good weather

☐ **Gosling**   German, English   little goose

☐ **Jarek**   Slavic   spring

☐ **Kelby**   English   dweller at the farm by the spring

☐ **Laverne**   French   springlike, the alder tree

☐ **Newlin**   Welsh   new pond

☐ **Solstice**   English from Latin   where the sun stands still

☐ **Verna**   Latin   springtime

STEPH'S FAVORITES

Popular

☐	**Arlo**	Irish, English	between two hills, fortified hill
☐	**Briar**	English	a thorny patch
☐	**Claire**	French	bright, clear
☐	**Fallon**	Irish	leader
☐	**Genevieve**	French	women of the race, white wave
☐	**Isla**	Scottish, Spanish	island
☐	**James**	Hebrew	supplanter
☐	**Penelope**	Greek	weaver
☐	**Piper**	English	one who plays the pipes or flute
☐	**Poppy**	English from Latin	red flower

<u>Uncommon</u>

☐ **Callum**	Scottish from Latin	dove
☐ **Corliss**	English	carefree person
☐ **Dashiell**	French surname	unknown
☐ **Dalerie**	invented	unknown
☐ **Forest**	French	woodsman or woods
☐ **Ophelia**	Greek	helper
☐ **Quill**	Irish, English	scribe, writer with a quill pen
☐ **Sonder**	Invented	the realization that each random passerby is living a life as vivid and complex as your own
☐ **Story**	Old Norse, Amer	tale
☐ **Verlice**	unclear	unclear

STRENGTH

Popular

☐	**Andrew**	Greek	strong and manly
☐	**Arnold**	German	eagle power
☐	**Brianna**	Irish	strong, virtuous, honorable
☐	**Ethan**	Hebrew	strong, firm
☐	**Gabriel**	Hebrew	God is my strength
☐	**Gertrude**	German	spear of strength
☐	**Keren**	Hebrew	strength, power, ray of light
☐	**Matilda**	German	strength in battle
☐	**Valentino**	Latin	strength, health
☐	**Valerie**	French from Latin	strength, health

<u>Uncommon</u>

☐	**Armstrong**	English, Scottish	strong arms
☐	**Burke**	English	from the fortress
☐	**Evander**	Greek	strong man, good man
☐	**Imre**	Hungarian	strength
☐	**Kenzo**	Japanese	strong and healthy, wise one
☐	**Maynard**	German	hardy, brave, strong
☐	**Nerio**	Latin from Greek	strength, valor
☐	**Philomena**	Greek	lover of strength
☐	**Senoda**	Basque	strength
☐	**Zale**	Greek	sea-strength

SUMMER

Popular

☐	**August**	German from Latin	great, magnificent, venerable
☐	**Evening**	Old English	period of time at the end of the day
☐	**Florence**	Latin	flourishing
☐	**Leo**	Latin	lion
☐	**Melissa**	Latin	honeybee
☐	**Ray**	German	wise protector
☐	**Rider**	English	horseman
☐	**Samson**	Hebrew	sun
☐	**Storm**	English	tempest
☐	**Summer**	English	summer

<u>Uncommon</u>

☐	**Enver**	Turkish	luminous
☐	**Grian**	Irish	the sun
☐	**Helios**	Greek	sun
☐	**Paradise**	English or Arabic	garden park or heaven
☐	**Raiden**	Japanese	thunder and lightning
☐	**Ravi**	Hindu	Hindu sun god, conferring
☐	**Salana**	Latin	sun
☐	**Senna**	Arabic	brightness
☐	**Sorley**	Irish	a summer sailor
☐	**Thor**	Norse	thunder

SURNAMES

Popular

☐	**Anderson**	English	son of Andrew/Anders
☐	**Bentley**	English	meadow with coarse grass
☐	**Briggs**	English	dweller by the bridge
☐	**Dawson**	English	son of David
☐	**Hayes**	English	hedged area
☐	**Jensen**	Scandinavian	son of Jens
☐	**Mackenzie**	Scottish	son of Kenneth
☐	**Rhodes**	Greek	a clearing in the woods, field of roses
☐	**Sullivan**	Irish	dark eyes
☐	**Sutton**	English	from the southern homestead

<u>Uncommon</u>

☐	**Ashford**	English	lives by the ash tree ford
☐	**Barlowe**	English	bare hillside
☐	**Colson**	English and Greek	son of Nicholas, swarthy, coal-black, charcoal
☐	**Delaney**	Irish	dark challenger
☐	**Mercer**	Old French	merchant
☐	**Palmer**	English	one who holds the palm, pilgrim
☐	**Stockard**	English	tree stump
☐	**Tilden**	English	from the fertile valley
☐	**Winthrop**	English	friend's village
☐	**Zimmerman**	German	carpenter

TERMS OF ENDEARMENT

Popular

☐	**Babs**	Latin	foreign woman
☐	**Buddy**	English	friend
☐	**Dolly**	English	gift of God
☐	**Honey**	Old English	nectar, sweet
☐	**Junior**	Latin	the younger on
☐	**Kitten**	English, Greek	young cat, pure
☐	**Peach**	Latin	Persian fruit
☐	**Peanut**	English	ground legume
☐	**Sonny**	English	son
☐	**Sweetie**	Old English	sweet or gentle person

<u>Uncommon</u>

☐ **Buster** — English from Latin — clumsy bird

☐ **Buttercup** — English — yellow wildflower

☐ **Buzz** — American — village in the woods

☐ **Candy** — Latin, English — white, pure, sincere, sweet

☐ **Chip** — English, French — free man

☐ **Darling** — English — dear

☐ **Poppet** — Middle English — small child or doll

☐ **Pumpkin** — Greek — large melon

☐ **Skipper** — English — captain

☐ **Sunshine** — English — light from the sun

THREE LETTERS

Popular

☐ **Ava**   Latin/Germanic   island, water, bird

☐ **Amy**   French   beloved

☐ **Cam**   Scottish   crooked nose

☐ **Dax**   French   leader

☐ **Eli**   Hebrew   ascended, uplifted, high

☐ **Lia**   Italian   weary

☐ **Mae**   English   bitter or pearl

☐ **Roy**   French or Celtic   king or red

☐ **Sue**   English   lily

☐ **Tim**   Greek   honoring God

<u>Uncommon</u>

☐	**Coe**	English surname	jackdaw bird
☐	**Fen**	Eng., Dutch/Frisian	marshland, peace
☐	**Fia**	Latin	flame
☐	**Kip**	Greek and Latin	bearer of Christ
☐	**Neo**	Latin or Tswana	new or gift
☐	**Oba**	African	king
☐	**Ora**	Latin	prayer
☐	**Pax**	Latin	peace
☐	**Tad**	Aramaic	gift of God
☐	**Van**	Dutch	of

TREES

<u>Popular</u>

☐	**Aspen**	Old English	shaking tree
☐	**Cedar**	Latin	cedar tree
☐	**Cypress**	English	cypress tree
☐	**Elowen**	Cornish	elm tree
☐	**Hollis**	English	dweller near the holly bushes
☐	**Juniper**	Latin	young
☐	**Lennox**	Scottish	elm grove
☐	**Nash**	English	dweller by the ash tree
☐	**Oakley**	English	meadow of oak trees
☐	**Willow**	English	willow tree

<u>Uncommon</u>

☐ **Arbor**	Latin	tree
☐ **Balsam**	German	seller of spices
☐ **Birch**	English	birch tree
☐ **Danner**	German	dweller near the fig tree
☐ **Elwood**	English	elder tree forest
☐ **Grove**	English	group of trees
☐ **Idra**	Aramaic	fig tree
☐ **Maple**	English from Latin	maple tree, piece of cloth
☐ **Perry**	English	dweller by the pear tree
☐ **Spruce**	varied	unknown

VICTORIAN

Popular

☐	**Alice**	German	noble
☐	**Amos**	Hebrew	carried by God
☐	**Annette**	French	grace
☐	**Edith**	English	prosperous in war
☐	**Edward**	English	guardian
☐	**Henry**	German	estate ruler
☐	**George**	Greek	farmer
☐	**Lydia**	Greek	woman from Lydia, Greece
☐	**Richard**	German	brave ruler
☐	**William**	German	resolute protection

Uncommon

☐ **Archibald** German truly brave, bold

☐ **Clarence** Latin bright

☐ **Cuthbert** English famous, brilliant

☐ **Effie** Greek pleasant speech

☐ **Enoch** Hebrew dedicated

☐ **Eugenia** Greek well born

☐ **Melvin** English council protector

☐ **Phineas** Hebrew Nubian

☐ **Sybil** Greek prophetess

☐ **Winston** English wine's town

VINTAGE

Popular

- [ ] **Albert** — German — noble, bright
- [ ] **Blanche** — French — white
- [ ] **Dorothy** — English from Greek — gift of God
- [ ] **Eleanor** — French — unknown
- [ ] **Emma** — German — universal
- [ ] **Harold** — Scandinavian — army ruler
- [ ] **Harvey** — French — battle worthy
- [ ] **Oscar** — Irish — deer lover
- [ ] **Virginia** — Latin — virginal, pure
- [ ] **Walter** — German — army ruler

Uncommon

☐ **Abner**   Hebrew   father of light

☐ **Chester**   Latin   fortress, walled town

☐ **Della**   German   noble

☐ **Etta**   English   ruler of the home

☐ **Gladys**   Welsh   land, country

☐ **Leory**   French   the king

☐ **Marmaduke**   Irish   devotee of Maedoc

☐ **Maude**   German   battle-mighty

☐ **Otis**   English, German   wealthy

☐ **Vernon**   English   place of alders

VIRTUE

<u>Popular</u>

☐	**Charity**	English	giving, kindness
☐	**Faith**	English	to trust
☐	**Grace**	English, Latin	charm, goodness, generosity
☐	**Hope**	English	desire of fulfillment
☐	**Joy**	Latin	happiness
☐	**Love**	English	deep affection
☐	**Peace**	English	tranquility
☐	**Prudence**	English, Latin	cautious, intelligent
☐	**Sincere**	American	honest
☐	**Truly**	English	honestly

<u>Uncommon</u>

☐ **Benevolent**	Old French	a desire to do good
☐ **Constance**	English	steadfastness
☐ **Honor**	English	dignity, reputation
☐ **Patience**	English	enduring or forbearing
☐ **Precious**	Latin	of great worth, expensive
☐ **Serendipity**	English	unexpected good fortune
☐ **Serenity**	English, Latin	peaceful
☐ **Temperance**	English	moderation, self-control
☐ **Verity**	Latin	truth
☐ **Winsome**	English	agreeable, lighthearted

WATER

Popular

☐	**Brook**	English	small stream
☐	**Caspian**	Latin	white
☐	**Harbor**	English	lodging for ships
☐	**Lake**	English	body of water
☐	**Marina**	Latin	from the sea
☐	**Nile**	Irish	champion
☐	**Ocean**	Greek	sea
☐	**Reef**	Old Norse	narrow rock ridge underwater
☐	**River**	English	flowing body of water
☐	**Sailor**	German	boat man

<u>Uncommon</u>

☐	**Adriatic**	Latin	of or relating to the sea that lies east of Italy
☐	**Baltic**	Latin	dwellers near the
☐	**Cascade**	French	small waterfall
☐	**Coast**	English	land near the sea
☐	**Indra**	Sanskrit	possessing drops of rain
☐	**Laguna**	Latin, Spanish	shallow body of water
☐	**Nerissa**	Greek	sea nymph, from the sea
☐	**Pacific**	Latin	tranquil
☐	**Tide**	Latin	knowledge of elevation, rhythm of the ocean
☐	**Wave**	Old English	swell on the surface of the water

WELSH

Popular

- ☐ **Bryn** — Welsh — hill
- ☐ **Dylan** — Welsh — son of the sea
- ☐ **Ellis** — Welsh, English — benevolent
- ☐ **Guinevere** — Welsh — white shadow, white wave
- ☐ **Lynn** — Welsh — lake
- ☐ **Rhonda** — Welsh — noisy one
- ☐ **Rhys** — Welsh — ardor
- ☐ **Tegan** — Welsh — fair
- ☐ **Trevor** — Welsh — from the large village
- ☐ **Winifred** — Welsh, Engilsh — blessed peacemaking

<u>Uncommon</u>

☐	**Anwen**	Welsh	very fair, beautiful
☐	**Caddock**	Welsh	eagerness for war
☐	**Dewey**	Welsh	beloved
☐	**Eira**	Welsh	snow
☐	**Esylit**	Welsh	fair lady
☐	**Fflur**	Welsh	flower
☐	**Glynis**	Welsh	small glen, valley
☐	**Nolwenn**	Welsh	shining, holy
☐	**Rhiannon**	Welsh	divine queen
☐	**Yale**	Welsh	fertile ground

WINTER

Popular

	Name	Origin	Meaning
☐	**Angel**	Greek	messenger
☐	**Carol**	English from Latin	free person or song
☐	**Estelle**	French	star
☐	**Gloria**	Latin	glory
☐	**Holiday**	English	holy day
☐	**Holly**	English	holly tree
☐	**Ivy**	English	climbing vine plant
☐	**Lucia**	Italian	light
☐	**Natasha**	Russian	born on Christmas or birthday of the Lord
☐	**Noelle**	French	Christmas

<u>Uncommon</u>

☐ **Barack**   Arabic, Swahili   blessed

☐ **Frost**   English   freezing

☐ **Glacier**   French   ice

☐ **Glow**   English   shine softly

☐ **Lodge**   English   shelter

☐ **Lumi**   Finnish   snow

☐ **Neve**   Irish   snow, bright

☐ **Rudolph**   German   famous wolf

☐ **Vesper**   Latin   evening star

☐ **Yuki**   Japanese   snow

Popular

☐	**Acre**	English	unit of land area
☐	**Bliss**	English	joy, cheer, intense happiness
☐	**Brick**	varied	mason, good guy, block of clay
☐	**Chance**	French	chancellor, good fortune
☐	**Eleven**	English	spelling of the number eleven
☐	**Gravity**	Latin	weight, heaviness, importance
☐	**Karma**	Hindi	destiny, fate, spiritual force
☐	**Lane**	English	small roadway or path
☐	**Legend**	English	hero, fable, myth
☐	**Poet**	English	one who writes verse

<u>Uncommon</u>

☐	**Abacus**	Greek	counting table
☐	**Chambray**	French	cotton blended material
☐	**Copper**	English	reddish-brown mineral, metal
☐	**Danger**	English	one who takes great risks
☐	**Imagery**	French	pictures or photographs
☐	**Julep**	Eng. From Persian	sweet drink or rose water
☐	**Kismet**	Arabic	fate
☐	**Theory**	Latin	idea, speculation
☐	**Velvet**	English	soft fabric
☐	**Whimsey**	English	playfulness in a unique manner of fancy

EPILOGUE

LET'S TALK ABOUT BABY naming advice. My suggestion is to make a short list of names you really, really like. Have your partner make a similar list and then edit them down to a short list of mutually favorite names. If still, nothing is speaking to you, nothing makes your heart flutter, or you and your partner cannot agree, try out each name on your list for a whole day or more. Speak about your child as if they are here, get their name on a coffee cup to see what it looks like, write it out with your last name, casually mention them in conversation ALL day and see how you feel. If you wrinkle your nose or forget to use the name, that will say a lot, and the ones that jump out to you will be your top contenders.

If you know in your gut the name you want to use for your child, but something is holding you back, I'd encourage you to explore exactly what is holding you back. Is it the nickname possibilities, the initials, the family member or friend who already has that moniker, the popularity of the name, or the uniqueness of the name? When you know what is bothering you, talk to a trusted and non-judgmental confidant to figure out if that should really be stopping you or if it is something you can get past.

For example, if you love Olivia, can you picture your child

being one of multiple Olivias in school or at soccer practice? Does that change your feelings? Or, if you love the name Birch, can you picture your son's friends asking him why he's named after a tree and him having to explain it? There is no right answer here; if you love your child's name and can explain to them how special it is and why you chose it, that is enough.

My least favorite comment is when people tell you your child will be bullied for having an uncommon name. Not only is it out of the child's control whether they are bullied or not, but we have to stop expecting everyone in society to fit into the same-sized boxes. The responsibility should lie in teaching our children to accept others regardless of their name, appearance, personality, etc., instead of making fun of those who are different from us. While there are definitely names that would be bad to give to a child, bullying is never OK, and we should not use it as a threat.

Thanks to the online world our names are used in so many places from email addresses to social media handles to personal brands. This means you are absolutely correct if you feel like naming a human is a big and daunting task. In fact, there is always time to buy a monogrammed blanket, so I encourage you to wait until your baby is born to make a final decision. Ideally you want to take that small list of five or fewer names to your place of birth and meet your child before committing to their name.

No matter what you do, don't panic. Give yourself time to fall in love with lots of names, and space to change your mind once or twice. Enjoy the search and share it with someone you trust. I have faith that you will do your best with the information you have at the time. Names are subjective, but the more I study them, pair them up, and say them out loud, the more beauty I have found in every single name.

FAVORITE NAMES

FAVORITE NAMES

FAVORITE NAMES

FAVORITE NAMES

FAVORITE NAMES

NAME INDEX

Aleah	ˈælə	80
Alexander	ˌæləgˈzændər	48
Alice	ˈæləs	112
Alina	əˈlinə	91
Alisdair	ˈælɪzdə	87
Almond	ˈɑmənd	40
Aloe	ˈæˌloʊ	71
Altan	ɔˈltn	19
Althea	ælˈθiə	25
Alvin	ˈælvɪn	67
Amanda	əˈmændə	64
Amari	ɑˈmɑri	55
Amber	ˈæmbər	16
Ambrose	ˈæmˌbroʊz	66
Ambrosia	æmˈbroʊʒə	41
Amethyst	ˈæmɪθɪst	44
Amos	ˈeɪməs	112
Amy	ˈeɪmi	108
Anacita	ænæsɪtə	93
Anakin	æneɪkɪn	57
Anders	ˈændərz	74
Anderson	ˈændərsən	104
Andrew	ˈændru	100
Anemone	əˈnɛməni	13
Angel	ˈeɪndʒəl	122
Anise	ˈænəs	94
Annette	əˈnɛt	112
Anthony	ˈænθəni	60
Antoinette	ˌæntwəˈnɛt	42
Anton	ˈænˌtɔn	90
Antonella	æntənlə	18
Anwen	ænwen	121

Aoife	ɔɪaɪf	59
Apollo	əˈpalou	50
Apple	ˈæpəl	40
April	ˈeɪprəl	96
Arabella	ˌærəˈbɛlə	33
Araceli	æɹɪlɪ	83
Arata	aˈratə	19
Arbor	ˈarbər	111
Archer	ˈartʃər	76
Archibald	ˈartʃəˌbɔld	113
Arcturus	ɑːrkˈtʊrəs	15
Argo	ˈargou	51
Aria	ˈariə	68
Ariel	ˈɛriəl	36
Aristotle	ˈɛrəˌstatəl	49
Arlette	ˌarˈlɛt	43
Arlo	ɑːɹ.lou	98
Armani	ˌarˈmani	81
Armstrong	ˈarmˌstraŋ	101
Arnold	ˈarnəld	100
Arsenio	ˌarˈsiniou	92
Artemis	aˈtmɪs	50
Asgard	əsgaˈd	75
Ash	æʃ	72
Ashby	ˈæʃbi	35
Asher	ˈæʃər	52
Ashford	ˈæʃfərd	105
Aspen	ˈæspən	110
Aster	ˈæstər	15
Astrid	ˈæstrɪd	75
Athena	əˈθinə	50
Atlas	ˈætləs	14
Atticus	ˈætɪkəs	49

Aubin	ˈɔbɪn	43
Audra	ɔˈdɹə	24
Audrey	ˈɔdri	78
August	ˈɑgəst	102
Aurelius	ɔˈəlɪəs	61
Aurora	əˈrɔrə	18
Austen	ˈɔstən	62
Austin	ˈɔstɪn	26
Autumn	ˈɔtəm	16
Ava	ˈeɪvə	108
Avalon	ˈævəˌlɑn	41
Avery	ˈeɪvəri	34
Avi	ˈɑvi	55
Aviva	ævivə	97
Axel	ˈæksəl	74
Azalea	əˈzeɪljə	39
Aziz	əˈziz	64
Azul	æʒuˈl	29
Babs	bæbz	106
Baldur	balˈdʊr	75
Balsam	ˈbɔlsəm	111
Baltic	ˈbɔltɪk	119
Barack	bɹæk	123
Barlowe	ˈbarˌloʊ	105
Barnabas	ˈbarnəbəs	21
Bartholomew	barˈθaləmˌju	33
Baruska	baˈɹʌskə	91
Basil	ˈbæzəl	94
Bay	beɪ	95
Bayless	ˈbeɪlɪs	77
Bear	bɛr	12
Beatrice	ˈbiətrəs	52

Becker	ˈbɛkər	76
Beckett	ˈbɛkɪt	62
Bee	bi	12
Belle	bɛl	36
Belladonna	ˈbɛləˈdɑnə	67
Bellona	bɛləʊnə	85
Benedict	ˈbɛnəˌdɪkt	60
Benevolent	bəˈnɛvələnt	117
Benjamin	ˈbɛndʒəmən	54
Bennett	ˈbɛnət	82
Bentley	ˈbɛntli	104
Benvolio	bɛnvɒliəʊ	89
Berry	ˈbɛri	40
Beryl	ˈbɛrəl	45
Bethel	ˈbɛθəl	55
Bianca	biˈɑŋkə	88
Bijou	baɪd͡ʒ	43
Birch	bɜrtʃ	111
Birdie	ˈbɜrdi	96
Birger	ˈbɜrdʒər	75
Bjorn	bjɔrn	74
Blake	blɛɪk	30
Blanche	blæntʃ	114
Blaze	blɛɪz	16
Bleu	blu	28
Bliss	blɪs	124
Blodwyn	blɒdwɪn	39
Blossom	ˈblɑsəm	38
Blythe	blaɪð	52
Booker	ˈbʊkər	24
Boone	bun	66
Boris	bɒɹɪs	90
Boston	bɒstən	26

Boswell	bɑzwɛl	35
Brahms	brɑmz	68
Bramble	ˈbræmbəl	71
Brando	ˈbrændoʊ	79
Brandy	ˈbrændi	40
Branwen	bɹænwen	23
Breccan	bɹekæn	59
Breeze	briz	70
Brianna	briˈænə	100
Briar	ˈbraɪər	98
Brick	brɪk	124
Briggs	brɪgz	104
Brigid	bɹɪd͡ʒɪd	58
Briley	ˈbrɪli	56
Brisa	bɹiˈzə	93
Brody	ˈbroʊdi	86
Bronte	ˈbrɑnti	63
Brook	brʊk	118
Bryn	brɪn	120
Buck	bʌk	12
Buddy	ˈbʌdi	106
Burke	bɜrk	101
Buster	ˈbʌstər	107
Buttercup	ˈbʌtərˌkʌp	107
Buzz	bʌz	107
Byron	ˈbaɪrən	62
Caddock	ˈkædək	121
Cadeau	kædəʊ	43
Cadence	ˈkeɪdəns	68
Cadmus	ˈkædməs	51
Cal	kæl	72
Caledonia	ˌkæləˈdoʊniə	33

Calgary	ˈkælgəri	26
Calla	ˈkælə	39
Calliope	kəˈlaɪəˌpi	51
Callista	kɔ:lɪstə	48
Callum	ˈkæləm	99
Cam	kæm	108
Campbell	ˈkæmbəl	86
Canary	kəˈnɛri	23
Candy	ˈkændi	107
Cantata	ˌkænˈtɑtə	69
Canyon	ˈkænjən	71
Caradoc	kæɹædɒk	65
Caraway	ˈkærəˌweɪ	95
Carden	ˈkɑrdən	77
Carissa	kaˈrisə	47
Carlos	ˈkɑrloʊs	92
Carmen	ˈkɑrmən	93
Carmine	ˈkɑrmən	142
Carol	ˈkærəl	122
Caroline	ˈkɛrəˌlaɪn	32
Carter	ˈkɑrtər	76
Carys	ˈkɛriz	65
Cascade	kæˈskeɪd	119
Cason	ˈkæsən	56
Caspian	ˈkæspiən	118
Cassius	kæsiəs	88
Castle	ˈkæsəl	37
Catalina	ˌkætəˈlinə	93
Cayenne	ˌkaɪˈɛn	94
Cecelia	sɪˈsiljə	60
Cedar	ˈsidər	110
Celestial	səˈlɛsʧəl	15
Celine	səˈlin	42

Ceres	ˈsɪriz	85
Cerise	səˈris	41
Chambray	tʃeɪmbɹeɪ	125
Chance	tʃæns	124
Chara	ˈtʃɑrə	53
Charity	ˈtʃɛrɪti	116
Charlie	ˈtʃɑrli	78
Charlotte	ˈʃɑrlət	42
Charm	tʃɑrm	67
Chartreuse	ʃɑrˈtruz	29
Chase	tʃeɪs	30
Cher	ʃɛr	64
Chessa	tʃesə	91
Chester	ˈtʃɛstər	115
Chip	tʃɪp	107
Chloris	ˈklɔrɪs	97
Christo	ˈkrɪstoʊ	90
Cinnamon	ˈsɪnəmən	95
Claire	klɛr	98
Clarabelle	ˈklærəbəl	82
Clarence	ˈklɛrəns	113
Clark	klɑrk	78
Claudette	kloʊˈdɛt	79
Clay	kleɪ	70
Clementine	ˈklɛmənˌtaɪn	143
Clove	klʌv	94
Clover	ˈkloʊvər	71
Coast	koʊst	119
Cocoa	ˈkoʊkoʊ	41
Coe	koʊ	109
Colson	ˈkoʊlsən	105
Colt	koʊlt	12

Comet	ˈkɑmət	14
Conor	ˈkɑnər	58
Constance	ˈkɑnstəns	117
Cooper	ˈkupər	76
Copper	ˈkɑpər	125
Corbin	ˈkɔrbɪn	22
Coretta	kəˈrɛtə	24
Coriander	ˌkɔriˈændər	95
Corliss	ˈkɔrlɪs	99
Cormac	ˈkɔrmək	59
Cornelius	kɔrˈniljəs	21
Corwin	ˈkɔrwɪn	65
Cosima	koʊˈsimə	49
Cosmos	ˈkɑzmoʊs	14
Cressida	kɹɛsaɪə	89
Crimson	ˈkrɪmzən	28
Crispin	ˈkrɪspɪn	17
Cruz	kruz	92
Crystal	ˈkrɪstəl	44
Cupid	ˈkjupɪd	85
Cuthbert	ˈkʌθbərt	113
Cyan	saɪˈæn	29
Cybele	sɪbiˈl	67
Cypress	ˈsaɪprəs	110
Cyril	ˈsɪrəl	49
Cyrus	ˈsaɪrəs	80
Daenerys	deɪɛnɹɪs	57
Daffodil	ˈdæfəˌdɪl	39
Dagan	ˈdeɪgən	17
Dagny	dægnɪ	19
Daisy	ˈdeɪzi	38
Dalerie	deɪləɹɪ	99
Dallas	ˈdæləs	26

Damaris	dəˈmɑrəs	21
Damek	dæmk	91
Damien	ˈdeɪmiən	48
Danger	ˈdeɪndʒər	125
Danica	ˈdænɪkə	90
Danielle	ˌdæniˈɛl	54
Danner	ˈdænər	111
Daphne	ˈdæfni	49
Darcy	ˈdɑrsi	62
Darius	dəˈraɪəs	81
Darlene	ˈdɑrˌlin	64
Darling	ˈdɑrlɪŋ	107
Darren	ˈdɑrən	58
Dashiell	ˈdæʃil	99
David	ˈdeɪvɪd	64
Dawn	dɔn	18
Dawson	ˈdɔsən	104
Dax	dæks	108
Deacon	ˈdikən	76
Dean	din	78
Deborah	ˈdɛbərə	20
Decker	ˈdɛkər	77
Delaney	dəˈleɪni	105
Delano	dɪˈlɑnoʊ	43
Delilah	dəˈlaɪlə	54
Della	ˈdɛlə	115
Demeter	dɪˈmitər	50
Demetrius	dɪˈmitriəs	49
Denver	ˈdɛnvər	26
Denzel	ˈdɛnzəl	24
Desdemona	dezdəmɒnə	89
Desi	ˈdɛzi	73

Deveraux	ˈdɛvərou	33
Dewey	ˈdui	121
Diana	daɪˈænə	84
Diego	diˈeɪgou	92
Dionysus	dɪənɪsəs	51
Doe	dou	12
Dolce	ˈdoʊlˌʧeɪ	41
Dolly	ˈdɑli	106
Doris	ˈdɔrəs	79
Dorothy	ˈdɔrəθi	114
Dottie	ˈdɑti	72
Douglas	ˈdʌgləs	86
Dove	dʌv	22
Dover	ˈdoʊvər	27
Draco	ˈdreɪkou	66
Drake	dreɪk	12
Draper	ˈdreɪpər	77
Drew	dru	72
Drummer	ˈdrʌmər	68
Duncan	ˈdʌŋkən	87
Dusty	ˈdʌsti	31
Dylan	ˈdɪlən	120
Earl	ɜrl	31
Eartha	ˈɜrθə	79
Easton	ˈistən	31
Eben	ˈɛbən	55
Ebony	ˈɛbəni	28
Ecru	ˈɛkru	29
Edelweiss	ˈeɪdəlˌvaɪs	39
Eden	ˈidən	54
Edgar	ˈɛdgər	88
Edith	ˈidɪθ	112
Edward	ˈɛdwərd	112

Edwin	'ɛdwən	34
Effie	'ɛfi	113
Eira	ɹə	121
Eleanor	'ɛlənɔr	114
Elena	'ɛlənə	92
Eleven	ɪ'lɛvən	124
Elfrida	ɛl'fridə	35
Elga	ɪl'gɑ	91
Eli	'ilaɪ	72
Eliana	ɪlaɪ̯ænə	82
Elizabeth	ɪ'lɪzəbəθ	54
Ella	'ɛlə	24
Ellis	'ɛlɪs	120
Eloise	ɪ'lɔɪz	42
Elowen	ɪləʊɪn	110
Elphaba	ɛlfɑbə	57
Elsa	'ɛlsə	36
Elwood	'ɛlˌwʊd	111
Ember	'ɛmbər	70
Embla	ɪmblə	75
Emerald	'ɛmrəld	44
Emily	'ɛmɪli	62
Emma	'ɛmə	114
Enfys	ɪnfaɪ̯z	83
Enid	'inɪd	66
Enoch	'inək	113
Enver	envə	103
Eoin	ɔɪn	47
Ephron	'ɛfrən	21
Eric	'ɛrɪk	36
Ernest	'ɜrnəst	63
Eros	'ɪrɑs	51

Eskander	eskændə	80
Esme	ɛzm	64
Estelle	ɛˈstɛl	122
Esther	ˈɛstər	80
Esylit	ˈɛ.sɪłt	121
Ethan	ˈiθən	100
Etta	ˈɛtə	115
Eudora	juˈdɔrə	37
Eugenia	ˌjuˈdʒiniə	113
Euphemia	juˈfimiə	33
Eva	ˈeɪvə	96
Evan	ˈɛvən	46
Evander	ˌiˈvændər	101
Evangeline	ɪˈvændʒɪˌlaɪn	82
Evanthe	evændð	49
Evening	ˈivnɪŋ	102
Evensong	iˈvnsɒŋ	69
Evolet	iˈvəlet	56
Ewan	ˈjuən	87
Ezra	ˈɛzrə	20
Fable	ˈfeɪbəl	37
Fairweather	ˈfɛrˌwɛðər	97
Faith	feɪθ	116
Falcon	ˈfælkən	22
Fallon	ˈfælən	98
Fane	feɪn	53
Farhad	fəæ	81
Fawn	fɔn	12
Faye	feɪ	30
Felicity	fɪˈlɪsəti	52
Felix	ˈfilɪks	52
Femi	fiˈmɪ	65
Fen	fɛn	109

Fennel	ˈfɛnəl	95
Ferdinand	ˈfɜrdɪˌnænd	33
Fergus	ˈfɜrgəs	87
Fern	fɜrn	96
Fflur	fluˈɜˈ	121
Fia	faɪɪə	109
Fifi	ˈfifi	73
Figaro	ˈfɪgəˌroʊ	37
Finch	fɪntʃ	23
Finley	ˈfɪnli	58
Fiona	fiˈoʊnə	86
Fiorella	fiɔˈrɛlə	33
Fitzgerald	fɪtsˈdʒɛrəld	63
Flora	ˈflɔrə	84
Florence	ˈflɔrəns	102
Florent	flɒɹənt	38
Flynn	flɪn	36
Forest	ˈfɔrəst	99
Foster	ˈfɑstər	77
Fox	fɑks	12
Francesca	frænˈtʃɛskə	32
Fraser	ˈfreɪzər	40
Fred	frɛd	78
Fresco	ˈfrɛskoʊ	19
Freya	ˈfreɪə	74
Frigg	fɹɪgg	65
Frost	frɔst	123
Gabriel	ˈgeɪbriəl	100
Gabrielle	ˈgæbriɛl	42
Gage	geɪdʒ	43
Gaia	ˈgaɪə	70
Galileo	ˌgæləˈliːoʊ	15

Galway	ˈgɑlweɪ	27
Gandalf	ˈgændɔlf	66
Gardner	ˈgɑrdnər	35
Garland	ˈgɑrlənd	79
Garnet	ˈgɑrnət	45
Gaston	ˈgæstən	37
Gatsby	ˈgætsbi	63
Gavin	ˈgævɪn	22
Gemini	ˈdʒɛməˌnaɪ	61
Genesis	ˈdʒɛnəsəs	18
Geneva	dʒəˈnivə	27
Genevieve	ˈdʒɛnəˌviv	98
Genova	ˈdʒɛnoʊvə	57
George	dʒɔrdʒ	112
Georgia	ˈdʒɔrdʒə	30
Gershwin	ˈgɜrʃwɪn	69
Gertrude	ˈgɜrtrud	100
Giada	d͡ʒaɪdə	45
Gianna	d͡ʒaɪənə	46
Gilead	gɪˈlid	21
Ginger	ˈdʒɪndʒər	94
Glacier	ˈgleɪʃər	123
Gladys	ˈglædɪs	115
Gloria	ˈglɔriə	122
Glow	gloʊ	123
Glynis	ˈglɪnɪs	121
Godiva	gəˈdaɪvə	83
Gold	goʊld	44
Golden	ˈgoʊldən	17
Gosling	gəʊslɪŋ	97
Grace	greɪs	116
Graham	ˈgreɪəm	86
Granger	ˈgreɪndʒər	77

Granite	ˈgrænət	71
Gravity	ˈgrævəti	124
Gray	greɪ	28
Greer	grɪr	87
Gregory	ˈgrɛgəri	32
Greta	ˈgritə	78
Grian	grɹaɪɪən	103
Gretel	ˈgrɛtəl	36
Griffin	ˈgrɪfɪn	50
Grove	groʊv	111
Guinevere	gwɪnɪvɪə	120
Gunnar	ˈgʌnər	74
Gwen	gwɛn	72
Gwyneth	ˈgwɪnəθ	52
Hadley	ˈhædli	30
Halcyon	ˈhælsiən	23
Hamish	ˈhæmɪʃ	86
Hamlet	ˈhæmlət	89
Handel	ˈhændəl	68
Hank	hæŋk	30
Hans	hɑns	46
Harbor	ˈhɑrbər	118
Harmony	ˈhɑrməni	68
Harold	ˈhɛrəld	114
Harper	ˈhɑrpər	34
Harriet	ˈhɛriət	24
Harvest	ˈhɑrvəst	17
Harvey	ˈhɑrvi	114
Hawk	hɔk	22
Hawthorne	ˈhɔθɔrn	71
Hayes	heɪz	104
Heather	ˈhɛðər	38

Hector	'hɛktər	51
Helia	helɪə	15
Helios	'hili‚ɑs	103
Henrietta	‚hɛnri'ɛtə	32
Henry	'hɛnri	112
Hera	'hɪrə	50
Hermia	'hɜrmiə	89
Hermione	hɜ'mʃn	63
Hippolyta	hɪ'pɒlɪtə	89
Holden	'hoʊldən	62
Holiday	'halə‚deɪ	122
Hollis	'halɪs	110
Holly	'hali	122
Holmes	hoʊmz	34
Holt	hoʊlt	35
Homer	'hoʊmər	50
Honey	'hʌni	106
Honor	'ɑnər	117
Hooper	'hupər	76
Hope	hoʊp	116
Humphrey	'hʌmfri	79
Hunter	'hʌntər	16
Ian	'iən	46
Icarus	'ɪ‚kɜrəs	50
Ida	'aɪdə	25
Idra	aɪdɹə	111
Idris	aɪdɹɪs	25
Imagery	'ɪmədʒri	125
Imogen	'ɪməgən	88
Imre	'ɪmrə	101
Indigo	'ɪndə‚goʊ	28
Indra	ɪndɹə	119
Ingram	'ɪŋgrəm	23

Ingrid	ˈɪŋgrɪd	74
Inizio	ɪnaɪzʃəʊ	19
Innes	ˈɪnəs	87
Irelyn	aɪ̯əlɪn	57
Iridiana	aɪ̯ɪdɪənə	83
Iris	ˈaɪrəs	82
Isaac	ˈaɪzək	52
Isabel	ˈɪzəˌbɛl	92
Isaiah	ˌaɪˈzeɪə	20
Isla	ˈilə	98
Ivy	ˈaɪvi	122
Jack	d͡ʒæk	36
Jada	d͡ʒeɪdə	24
Jade	d͡ʒeɪd	44
Jagger	ˈd͡ʒægər	77
Jaguar	ˈd͡ʒæˌgwɑr	13
James	d͡ʒeɪmz	98
Jameson	ˈd͡ʒeɪmsən	34
Jane	d͡ʒeɪn	46
Janisa	d͡ʒæniˈzə	47
January	ˈd͡ʒænjuˌɛri	18
Janus	ˈd͡ʒeɪnəs	84
Jarek	d͡ʒeək	97
Jasmine	ˈd͡ʒæzmən	80
Jasper	ˈd͡ʒæspər	80
Jaxon	d͡ʒæksn	56
Jazz	d͡ʒæz	69
Jean	d͡ʒin	46
Jensen	ˈd͡ʒɛnsən	104
Jericho	ˈd͡ʒɛrɪˌkoʊ	21
Jesse	ˈd͡ʒɛsi	82
Jewel	ˈd͡ʒuəl	44

Joan	ʤoʊn	78
Joanna	ʤoʊˈænə	82
Joey	ˈʤoʊi	72
John	ʤɑn	46
Jolie	ˌʤoʊˈli	42
Jonah	ˈʤoʊnə	20
Jonesy	ʤ͡əʊnsɪ	47
Jora	ʤ͡ɔːɹə	17
Joseph	ˈʤoʊsəf	20
Jovan	ˈʤoʊvən	91
Jovie	ʤ͡əʊvɪ	56
Joy	ʤɔɪ	116
Joyce	ʤɔɪs	62
Judas	ˈʤudəs	48
Julep	ˈʤuləp	125
Julian	ˈʤuliən	60
Juliet	ˈʤuliˌɛt	88
June	ʤun	96
Junior	ˈʤunjər	106
Juniper	ˈʤunəpər	110
Juno	ˈʤunoʊ	84
Jupiter	ˈʤupətər	84
Kady	ˈkeɪdi	18
Kalasia	kəlæzʒɪə	47
Kale	keɪl	41
Karma	ˈkɑrmə	124
Kayden	keɪdʌn	56
Kayla	ˈkeɪlə	154
Kayvan	keɪvɑˈn	80
Keiko	ˈkeɪkoʊ	53
Kelby	ˈkɛlbi	97
Kelly	ˈkɛli	78
Kennedy	ˈkɛnədi	58

Kenzo	ˈkɛnzoʊ	101
Kepler	ˈkɛplər	15
Keren	keɹən	100
Kestrel	kestɹl	23
Keyne	kiˈn	83
Khaleesi	kheɪliˈɪzaɪ̯	57
Kia	ˈkiər	18
Kingsley	ˈkɪŋzli	34
Kingston	ˈkɪŋstən	33
Kinsey	ˈkɪnzi	31
Kip	kɪp	109
Kiran	kɪəɹən	82
Kirk	kɜrk	79
Kismet	ˈkɪzmɪt	125
Kit	kɪt	12
Kitten	ˈkɪtən	106
Lachlan	ˈlæklən	86
Laguna	ləˈgunə	119
Lainey	leɪniˈ	31
Lake	leɪk	118
Lala	ˈlɑlə	91
Landry	ˈlændri	43
Lane	leɪn	124
Langston	ˈlæŋstən	25
Lark	lɑrk	22
Lars	lɑrz	74
Lathan	ˈlæθən	57
Lavender	ˈlævəndər	38
Laverne	ləˈvɜrn	97
Lawrence	ˈlɔrəns	61
Leah	ˈliə	20
Lee	li	72

Legend	ˈlɛdʒənd	124
Leif	lif	96
Leila	ˈlilə	80
Lennon	ˈlɛnən	64
Lennox	ˈlɛnəks	110
Leo	ˈlioʊ	102
Leonardo	ˌliəˈnɑrdoʊ	32
Leroy	ˈliˌrɔɪ	115
Leta	ˈlɛtə	53
Lettie	ˈlɛti	73
Lev	lɛv	64
Levi	ˈlivaɪ	20
Lia	ˈliə	108
Liam	ˈliəm	58
Liber	ˈlɪbər	85
Libra	ˈlibrə	17
Lienna	len	47
Lilith	ˈlɪlɪθ	66
Lily	ˈlɪli	38
Link	lɪŋk	73
Linnea	ˈlɪniə	41
Liora	laɪˈɹəɹə	83
Liv	lɪv	74
Locket	ˈlɑkɪt	37
Lodge	lɑdʒ	123
Logan	ˈloʊgən	86
Lollie	lɒlɪ	40
Lonan	ləʊnæn	23
London	ˈlʌndən	26
Lourdes	lɔrdz	27
Love	lʌv	116
Lowry	ˈlaʊri	63
Luba	ˈlubə	65

Lucia	ˈluʃə	122
Lucina	luˈsɪnʌ	85
Lucy	ˈlusi	34
Lumi	lʌmɪ	123
Luna	ˈlunə	14
Lux	lʌks	61
Lydia	ˈlɪdiə	112
Lynn	lɪn	120
Lynx	lɪŋks	13
Lyra	ˈlaɪrə	68
Lysander	ˌlaɪˈsændər	89
Mabel	ˈmeɪbəl	31
Mack	mæk	73
Mackenzie	məˈkɛnzi	104
Mae	meɪ	108
Maeve	məˈɛv	58
Magdalena	ˌmægdəˈlinə	21
Mage	mæd͡ʒ	66
Magenta	məˈd͡ʒɛntə	29
Magnolia	mægˈnoʊljə	38
Maia	ˈmaɪə	84
Malcolm	ˈmælkəm	86
Maldue	mɔˈldjuˈ	67
Maple	ˈmeɪpəl	111
Marc	mɑrk	42
Marcella	mɑrˈsɛlə	61
Marigold	ˈmɛrəˌgoʊld	38
Marilyn	ˈmɛrələn	78
Marina	məˈrinə	118
Marisol	mæɹɪsəʊl	93
Maritza	mæɹɪtə	92
Marmaduke	ˈmɑrməˌduk	115

Mars	mɑrz	14
Martin	ˈmɑrtən	24
Mason	ˈmeɪsən	30
Matilda	məˈtɪldə	100
Maude	mɔd	115
Mauve	mɔv	28
Maven	ˈmeɪvən	55
Maverick	ˈmævərɪk	56
Maximilian	ˌmæksɪˈmɪliən	32
Maxon	ˈmæksən	56
May	meɪ	96
Maynard	ˈmeɪnərd	101
Mazarine	mæzeəɹɪn	29
McKenna	məˈkɛnə	86
Meadow	ˈmɛˌdoʊ	70
Medora	meɪˈdɔrə	49
Meg	mɛg	62
Melissa	məˈlɪsə	102
Melody	ˈmɛlədi	68
Melvin	ˈmɛlvɪn	113
Mercedes	mərˈseɪdiz	93
Mercer	ˈmɜrsər	105
Mercury	ˈmɜrkjəri	15
Merla	mlə	23
Mia	ˈmiə	72
Micah	ˈmaɪkə	54
Mickey	ˈmɪki	79
Mila	mələ	90
Milena	ˈmɪlɛna	64
Mimir	mɪmaɪə	75
Minerva	məˈnɜrvə	85
Mint	mɪnt	94
Miranda	məˈrændə	88

Mo	moʊ	73
Montague	ˈmɑntəˌgju	89
Montgomery	mɑntˈgʌmri	32
Moon	mun	70
Morag	mɔˈɹæg	87
Mosley	ˈmoʊzli	35
Moss	mɔs	71
Mozart	ˈmoʊzɑrt	68
Muhammad	mʊˈhaməd	28
Muriel	ˈmjʊriəl	59
Nadia	ˈnædjə	90
Nala	nlə	37
Naomi	neɪˈoʊmi	52
Nariman	nɑˈɹiˈmən	81
Nash	næʃ	110
Natasha	nəˈtɑʃə	112
Naveen	neɪviˈn	37
Navy	ˈneɪvi	28
Nelo	nɪləʊ	93
Neo	ˈnioʊ	109
Neoma	neɪˈoʊmə	19
Neon	ˈniɑn	18
Neptune	ˈnɛptun	84
Nerio	ˈnɛrioʊ	101
Nerissa	nəɹɪsə	119
Neve	ˈnɛveɪ	123
Neven	nevn	83
Newlin	ˈnulɪn	97
Niamh	niˈveɪ	59
Nile	naɪl	118
Nils	nɪlz	74
Ninette	nɪˈnɛt	47

Nixie	ˈnɪksi	67
Noah	ˈnoʊə	54
Noelle	noʊˈɛl	122
Noelani	nəʊələnɪ	83
Nolan	ˈnoʊlən	30
Nolwenn	nəlwen	121
Nona	ˈnɑnə	85
Nori	nəɹɪ	41
Nova	ˈnoʊvə	14
November	noʊˈvɛmbər	17
Oakley	ˈoʊkli	110
Oba	ˈoʊbə	109
Oberon	ˈoʊbəˌrɑn	89
Obi	ɒbɪ	65
Ocean	ˈoʊʃən	118
Octave	ˈɑktɪv	68
Octavia	ɑkˈteɪviə	16
October	ɑkˈtoʊbər	16
Odette	ˌoʊˈdɛt	43
Odin	ˈoʊdən	74
Ohanna	əʊhænə	47
Oisin	ɔɪzɪn	59
Oksana	ˌɑkˈsænə	90
Olive	ˈɑləv	40
Onni	ˈɑni	53
Onyx	ˈɑnɪks	45
Opal	ˈoʊpəl	44
Ophelia	əˈfiljə	99
Ora	ˈɔrə	109
Orion	oʊˈraɪən	14
Orlando	ɔrˈlændoʊ	26
Orli	ˈɔrlɪ	55
Oscar	ˈɔskər	114

Oswald	'ɔzwɔld	35
Otis	'oʊtɪs	115
Otter	'atər	13
Ottilie	'atəli	33
Pacific	pə'sɪfɪk	119
Padraig	pɑːrɪk	59
Paige	peɪdʒ	34
Paisley	peɪzlɪ	16
Pallas	'pæləs	51
Palmer	'pamər	105
Paloma	pa'loʊmə	93
Panda	'pændə	13
Paradise	'pɛrəˌdaɪs	103
Paris	'pɛrɪs	26
Parisa	pæɹi'zə	81
Parks	'pɑːrks	71
Parker	'pɑrkər	76
Parnell	pɑːr'nɛl	43
Patience	'peɪʃəns	117
Paul	pɔl	60
Pax	pæks	109
Peace	pis	116
Peach	pitʃ	106
Peanut	'pinət	106
Pearl	pɜrl	44
Pegasus	'pɛgəsəs	67
Penelope	pə'nɛləpi	98
Pepper	'pɛpər	94
Peridot	'pɛrɪdɔt	45
Perry	'pɛri	111
Petal	'pɛtəl	39
Peter	'pitər	48

Peyton	ˈpeɪtən	30
Philip	ˈfɪləp	36
Philomena	fɪləˈminə	101
Phineas	ˈfɪniəs	113
Phoebe	ˈfibi	48
Phoenix	ˈfinɪks	18
Pike	paɪk	13
Piper	ˈpaɪpər	98
Pippa	paɪpə	73
Pixie	ˈpɪksi	37
Pluto	ˈplutoʊ	84
Poe	poʊ	63
Poet	ˈpoʊət	124
Polaris	poʊˈlɛrəs	14
Pomona	poʊˈmoʊnə	61
Poppet	pɒpɪt	107
Poppy	ˈpɑpi	98
Porter	ˈpɔrtər	76
Portia	ˈpɔrʃə	88
Poseidon	pəˈsaɪdən	51
Posey	ˈpoʊzi	38
Precious	ˈprɛʃəs	117
Preeda	pɹiˈdə	53
Preston	ˈprɛstən	30
Primrose	ˈprɪmˌroʊz	96
Priscilla	prɪˈsɪlə	60
Priya	pɹaɪə	64
Prudence	ˈprudəns	116
Puck	pʌk	89
Puma	ˈpumə	13
Pumpkin	ˈpʌmpkɪn	107
Quartz	kwɔrts	45
Quill	kwɪl	99

Quince	kwɪns	41
Quinn	kwɪn	58
Quintin	ˈkwɪntɪn	61
Rachel	ˈreɪʧəl	20
Radcliff	ˈrædklɪf	35
Radley	ˈrædli	17
Raiden	ɹeɪdn	103
Raina	ˈreɪnə	90
Ramin	ɹæmɪn	81
Ranger	ˈreɪndʒər	43
Raphaela	ˈræfaɪˈɛlə	83
Rapunzel	ɹˈæpʌnzəl	37
Raven	ˈreɪvən	22
Ravi	ˌrɑˈvi	103
Ray	reɪ	102
Reef	rif	118
Regan	ˈrigən	88
Regin	ˌriˈdʒɪn	66
Remington	ˈrɛmɪŋtən	32
Remus	ˈriməs	85
Remy	ˈrɛmi	42
Ren	rɛn	39
Renee	rəˈneɪ	19
Reno	ˈrinoʊ	27
Revel	ˈrɛvəl	53
Reverie	ˈrɛvəri	67
Reza	ˈrɛzə	81
Rhapsody	ˈræpsədi	69
Rhea	ˈriə	49
Rhiannon	ɹhjənən	121
Rhodes	roʊdz	104
Rhonda	ˈrɑndə	120

Rhys	ris	120
Ricardo	rɪˈkɑrdoʊ	92
Richard	ˈrɪtʃərd	112
Rider	ˈraɪdər	102
Riley	ˈraɪli	58
Rio	ˈrioʊ	26
Rita	ˈritə	79
River	ˈrɪvər	118
Robin	ˈrɑbən	22
Robinson	ˈrɑbənsən	25
Rocco	ˈrɑkoʊ	56
Roman	ˈroʊmən	60
Romeo	ˈroʊmiˌoʊ	88
Rooster	ˈrustər	23
Roper	ˈroʊpər	77
Rory	ˈrɔri	16
Rosa	ˈroʊzə	24
Rosalind	ˈrɑzəlɪnd	88
Roscoe	ˈrɑskoʊ	71
Rose	roʊz	38
Rosemary	ˈroʊzˌmɛri	94
Rosetta	roʊˈzɛtə	80
Roux	ru	29
Roxanne	ˈrɑksɪn	80
Roy	rɔɪ	108
Ruby	ˈrubi	44
Rudolph	ˈrudɔlf	123
Rune	run	67
Russet	ˈrʌsɪt	29
Rust	rʌst	16
Ryker	ˈraɪkər	31
Sable	ˈseɪbəl	13
Saffron	ˈsæfrən	94

Sagan	ˈseɪgən	15
Sage	seɪdʒ	94
Sailor	ˈseɪlər	118
Salana	sælænə	103
Salem	ˈseɪləm	66
Salinger	ˈsɔlɪŋər	63
Salvador	ˈsælvəˌdɔr	92
Sam	sæm	72
Samson	ˈsæmsən	102
Samuel	ˈsæmjul	82
Sanna	ˈsænə	75
Santiago	ˌsæntiˈɑgoʊ	93
Saoirse	sˈɜːʃə	58
Sapphire	ˈsæfaɪər	44
Sara	ˈsɛrə	54
Savannah	səˈvænə	70
Sawyer	ˈsɔjər	76
Scarlet	ˈskɑrlət	28
Seal	sil	13
Sean	ʃɔn	46
Sebastian	səˈbæstʃən	36
Seeley	ˈsili	53
Seldon	ˈsɛldən	35
Selene	səˈlin	51
Senna	ˈsɛnə	103
Senoda	senɒdə	101
Serena	səˈrinə	60
Serenade	ˌsɛrəˈneɪd	69
Serendipity	ˌsɛrənˈdɪpɪti	117
Serenity	səˈrɛnəti	117
Sesame	ˈsɛsəmi	95
Shallot	ʃəˈlɒt	41

Shark	ʃɑrk	13
Sheena	ˈʃinə	46
Shelley	ˈʃɛli	62
Sherry	ˈʃɛri	40
Shifra	ʃifɹə	21
Shira	ˈʃɪrə	55
Shirin	ˈʃɪrən	81
Shirley	ˈʃɜrli	24
Sidney	ˈsɪdni	79
Sienna	siˈɛnə	28
Sierra	siˈɛrə	92
Signy	saɪ̯ni	75
Silas	ˈsaɪləs	60
Silver	ˈsɪlvər	45
Silvia	ˈsɪlviə	84
Sincere	sɪnˈsɪr	116
Sirius	sɹaɪ̯əs	15
Skipper	ˈskɪpər	107
Skye	skaɪ̯	14
Slate	sleɪt	70
Soleil	soʊˈleɪl	15
Solomon	ˈsɑləmən	55
Solstice	ˈsɔlstɪs	97
Sonder	sɒndə	99
Sonny	ˈsʌni	106
Sophia	soʊˈfiə	48
Soprano	səˈprɑnoʊ	69
Sorley	slɪ	103
Sparrow	ˈspɛroʊ	23
Spencer	ˈspɛnsər	76
Spruce	sprus	111
Stan	stæn	73
Stanislav	ˈstænɪslɑv	90

Starling	ˈstɑrlɪŋ	22
Stavros	stəˈvroʊz	49
Stella	ˈstɛlə	14
Stephanie	ˈstɛfəni	48
Stewart	ˈstuərt	78
Stockard	ˈstɑkərd	105
Storm	stɔrm	102
Story	ˈstɔri	99
Sue	su	108
Suki	ˈsuki	65
Sullivan	ˈsʌləvən	104
Summer	ˈsʌmər	102
Sunshine	ˈsʌn ʃaɪn	107
Sutton	ˈsʌtən	104
Sweetie	ˈswiti	106
Sybil	ˈsɪbɪl	113
Sylvia	ˈsɪlviə	61
Symphony	ˈsɪmfəni	69
Tabitha	ˈtæbɪθə	31
Tad	tæd	109
Tadhg	tædŋ	59
Taffy	ˈtæfi	40
Talitha	ˈtælɪðə	21
Tamarind	tæməɹɪnd	95
Tan	tæn	19
Tarana	tɑˈɹænə	25
Tate	teɪt	52
Tatiana	ˌtæˌtiˈænə	32
Tawny	ˈtɔːni	29
Taylor	ˈteɪlər	34
Tegan	tiˈgn	120
Temperance	ˈtɛmpərəns	117

Tempo	ˈtɛmˌpoʊ	69
Tennyson	ˈtɛnɪsən	63
Terra	ˈtɛrə	70
Theoden	θiːədən	57
Theodore	ˈθiəˌdɔr	48
Theory	ˈθɪri	125
Theseus	ðɪzɪs	51
Thirza	ˈθɜrzə	53
Thistle	ˈθɪsəl	71
Thor	θɔr	103
Thurgood	ˈθɜrgʊd	25
Thyme	θaɪm	95
Tiana	ʃənə	90
Tiberius	tɪbəɹaɪəs	85
Tibor	tɪbə	91
Tide	tˈaɪd	119
Tilden	ˈtɪldən	105
Tim	tɪm	108
Tinley	ˈtɪnli	56
Todrick	tɑdrɪk	57
Topaz	ˈtoʊˌpæz	45
Tove	təʊv	75
Trevor	ˈtrɛvər	120
Triton	ˈtraɪtən	50
Truly	ˈtruli	116
Tully	ˈtʌli	59
Ula	ˈjulə	45
Umber	ʌmbə	29
Una	ˈunə	61
Uziel	juˈzel	55
Vail	veɪl	27
Valentino	ˌvælənˈtinoʊ	100
Valerie	ˈvæləri	100

Van	væn	109
Vanellope	vənɛləp	57
Vanilla	vəˈnɪlə	95
Vanya	ˈvɑnjə	47
Vasco	ˈvæskoʊ	93
Vashti	ˈvæʃti	81
Velvet	ˈvɛlvət	125
Venus	ˈvinəs	84
Vera	ˈvɛrə	82
Verity	ˈvɛrəti	117
Verlice	vlɪs	99
Verna	ˈvɜrnə	97
Vernon	ˈvɜrnən	115
Verona	vəˈroʊnə	27
Vesper	ˈvɛspər	123
Vesta	ˈvɛstə	85
Victoria	vɪkˈtɔriə	60
Vienna	viˈɛnə	26
Viggo	vɪggəʊ	75
Violet	ˈvaɪəlɪt	28
Virginia	vərˈdʒɪnjə	114
Vivaldi	vɪˈvɑldi	69
Wagner	ˈwægnər	77
Walker	ˈwɔkər	31
Wallace	ˈwɔləs	87
Walter	ˈwɔltər	114
Warren	ˈwɔrən	42
Wave	weɪv	119
Wells	wɛlz	96
Wendy	ˈwɛndi	36
Wheatley	ˈwitli	17
Whimsy	ˈwɪmsi	125

Whistler	'wɪslər	77
Whitford	'wɪtfərd	35
Whitney	'wɪtni	25
Wilbur	'wɪlbər	62
William	'wɪljəm	112
Willoughby	'wɪləbi	33
Willow	'wɪˌloʊ	110
Winifred	'wɪnɪfrɪd	120
Winsome	'wɪnsəm	117
Winston	'wɪnstən	113
Winthrop	'wɪnθrəp	105
Wisteria	wɪstɪəɹɪə	39
Wolf	wʊlf	12
Wren	rɛn	22
Wylie	'waɪli	87
Wyn	wɪn	73
Yale	jeɪl	121
Yannick	'jænɪk	47
Yarrow	'jɑroʊ	95
York	jɔrk	27
Yuki	ju'kɪ	123
Zachary	'zækəri	54
Zale	zeɪl	101
Zane	zeɪn	46
Zaria	'zɑriə	27
Zarina	zeəɹi'nə	81
Zeke	zik	31
Zelda	'zɛldə	66
Zera	'zɛrə	19
Zeus	zus	50
Zimmerman	'zɪmərmən	105
Zimri	zɪmɹɪ	55
Zinnia	'zɪniə	39

Zipporah	zɪpəɹə	21
Ziven	zɪvn	91
Zoe	ˈzoʊi	48
Zora	ˈzɔrə	25
Zoran	ˈzɔrən	19
Zorina	zɔˈrinə	91
Zorion	zɔˈriən	53

ACKNOWLEDGEMENTS

My husband Iain. I'm beyond grateful for your unwavering dedication to my dreams. You're an amazing support system for me and the best father to our kiddos. You are the smartest, kindest, and cutest man I know. Life is better by your side.

My children, Euan, Fitz, and Orianna. Thank you for being my reason for everything and my daily source of joy. Being your mother is my forever favorite.

My parents, Vicky and Gene. You have no idea what your constant love and support have done for me. I truly believed I could do anything. And now I'm doing it. Thank you for giving me the space and safety to grow into the person I was meant to be, I'm proud to be your daughter.

My siblings, Melissa and Josh. I can feel your endless support and I'm so grateful to have only gotten closer to you both as the decades have passed. You guys inspire me to be better in all aspects of my life and I could not be more proud to be your sister.

My BFF, Laura. This book writing and publishing process would not have been possible with you. You listen and love me like a best friend should, but also motivate and guide me as the awesome business manager you are; thank you for always believing in me. I look forward to growing old together.

My extended family and friends. I am so grateful for each and every one of you. I see your love and support and I'm a better person because of it.

My TikTok community. You are the most thoughtful and amazing group. I wouldn't be here without all of you and I am forever grateful.

A special thank you to these online spaces for name inspiration and information:

Websites:

Nameberry.com

BabyNames.com

Behindthename.com

Blogs:

Appellationmountain.net

allthingsbabynames.com

Copy Editor, Proofreader, and IPA in Index: Bluetobliss on Fiverr

Cover Design: BBdesignstudio on Fiverr

Logo Design: Adripoggetti on Fiverr

Book Formatting: Catherine Downen

Beta Reader: Chelseaburdick on Fiverr

If you want Steph to be your name consultant or you just want to connect with her, you can find all the links you need on nameswithsteph.com